Better CEO-Board Relations

Better CEO-Board Relations

Practical Advice
for a Successful Partnership

∽

Karen Gardner

EDITOR

Health Forum, Inc.
An American Hospital Association Company
CHICAGO

This publication is designed to provide accurate and authoritative information in regard to the subject matter covered. It is sold with the understanding that neither the authors nor the publisher are engaged in rendering legal, accounting or other professional services. If legal advice or other expert assistance is required, the services of a competent professional should be sought.

The views expressed in this publication are strictly those of the authors and do not represent the official positions of the American Hospital Association.

AHA is a service mark of the American Hospital Association used under license by Health Forum, Inc.

Copyright © 2007 by Health Forum, Inc., an American Hospital Association company. All rights reserved. No part of this publication may be reproduced, stored in a retrieval system, or transmitted, in any form or by any means—electronic, mechanical, photocopying, recording, or otherwise—without the prior written permission of the publisher.

Printed in the United States of America—03/07

Cover design by Cheri Kusek

Library of Congress Cataloging-in-Publication Data
Better CEO-board relations : practical advice for a successful partnership / Karen Gardner.
    p. cm.
  Includes index.
  ISBN 978-1-55648-341-7 (paperback)
   1. Hospitals—Administration. 2. Hospital administrators. 3. Chief executive officers. 4. Directors of corporations. I. Gardner, Karen.

RA971.B48 2007
362.11068—dc22

2006049719

ISBN-10: 1-55648-341-4
ISBN-13: 978-1-55648-341-7   Item Number: 196901

Discounts on bulk quantities of books published by Health Forum, Inc., are available to professional associations, special marketers, educators, trainers, and others. For details and discount information, contact Health Forum, Inc., One North Franklin, 28th Floor, Chicago, IL 60606-3421 (Phone: 1-800-242-2626).

Contents

About the Editor	vii
Foreword *by George F. Lynn*	ix
Preface	xi

PART ONE   CEO RECRUITMENT

What Kind of CEO Will Your Hospital Need Next? A Model for Succession Planning *Andrew N. Garman and J. Larry Tyler*	3
Succession Planning: The Art of Transferring Leadership *Jordan Hadelman and Elaina Spitaels-Genser*	9
The Art of Interviewing Your Next CEO *David W. Thompson and Nancie Noie Thompson*	21
Managing CEO Transition *John R. Gardner*	31

PART TWO   COMMUNICATION

Behind Closed Doors: Should the Board Hold Executive Sessions? *Laurie Larson*	37
Tough Love: Ten Questions to Ask Your CEO *Paul B. Hofmann and Wanda J. Jones*	45
Executive Sessions as Standard Operating Procedure *Eric D. Lister, M.D., and Carolyn Jacoby Gabbay*	51

PART THREE CEO LEADERSHIP

Orchestrating the New Leadership: What It Takes
to Be a CEO Today *Patrick Plemmons* 59

Your CEO: Are You Short-Staffed or Shortsighted?
Laurie Larson 71

Leading by Listening: How Scripps Health Turned
Defeat Around *Laurie Larson* 79

PART FOUR THE BOARD CHAIR AND THE CEO

Side by Side: Communication Is Key to a Successful
CEO–Board Chair Partnership *Jan Greene* 91

Synergy in Motion: The Board Chair and CEO
Relationship *Elizabeth D. Becker-Reems* 101

PART FIVE EXECUTIVE COMPENSATION

CEO Measurement and Evaluation: The Three P's
Claudia Wyatt-Johnson and Edward Bancroft 115

Calibrating Executive Compensation
Claudia Wyatt-Johnson and Christopher J. Bennett 121

Avoiding Scandal: Recommended Practices for Board
Executive Compensation Committees
*Michael W. Peregrine, Ralph E. DeJong
and Timothy J. Cotter* 131

Index 141

About the Editor

Karen Gardner has been a health care editor for more than 20 years—as editor of *Trustee* magazine since 1989 and, prior to that, as executive editor of periodicals for the Joint Commission on Accreditation of Healthcare Organizations (JCAHO). Before entering the health care field, Gardner edited several legal publications.

Gardner writes a monthly column in *Trustee,* has published numerous articles in the magazine and is the editor of two books—a book on quality in hospice care, published by the JCAHO, and a book on hospital governance, published by AHA Press.

Gardner shepherded a major redesign of *Trustee* in 1995, and under her editorial direction, the magazine has won a number of editorial and graphic awards—from the Society of National Association Publications (including a Gold Award for General Excellence), from the American Society of Business Press Editors and from the American Society of Healthcare Publication Editors.

Gardner received a master of arts in teaching (M.A.T.) English from the University of Chicago, and before entering the editorial field, taught English at the high school and middle school levels in Chicago.

Foreword

While writing these words, I am reflecting on a 20-year career as CEO of a regional health system. As I think about my connection to the many trustees who have served our organization, I am struck by the fact that, in all those years, my relationship with hundreds of trustees has been held together by one common thread: service to others. This is truly remarkable when you stop to think about it.

One of our retired chairmen makes the point that "there is no more important charitable organization in the community than the hospital. There is no single place which does more to help people—the sick, the injured and the poor. It is a privilege to serve people in need as a trustee of such an important endeavor." I think hospital trustees across America would agree with him.

The notion of service to those in need is a powerful force. It galvanizes most people who serve on not-for-profit boards. And it provides focus to the important partnership between trustees and their CEOs.

A unique synergy is required between CEOs and the trustees who chair their hospital boards. This synergy is a dynamic give and take that is necessary to ensure that hospitals meet their obligations to the communities they serve. Those relationships do not happen without work.

At first glance, the notion of a volunteer board of community leaders providing management oversight and policy direction for an organization as complex as a hospital does not seem like a very good idea. The board may not understand completely the business that it is overseeing.

But as we know, trustees bring more to the board table than management oversight. They bring their knowledge and connection to the community, making sure that the effective operation of the "business" of health care enables the work of caring and curing. Good board-CEO relationships allow this balance to occur. Without it, the hospital runs the risk of becoming just another business.

In *Better CEO-Board Relations: Practical Advice for a Successful Partnership*, Karen Gardner has assembled a collection of articles from *Trustee* magazine that can help build stronger relationships between CEOs and their boards. Covering such topics as recruitment, communication, leadership and compensation, Ms. Gardner introduces us to experts in the field and some best practices that can be put to use in your hospital. This book is an excellent resource for trustees and hospital executives who wish to tighten the connections between board and management and improve organizational performance.

George F. Lynn

President
AtlantiCare
Atlantic City, New Jersey

Immediate Past Chair
American Hospital Association

Preface

Among all the important responsibilities that health care boards have, those with the greatest impact on the board's ability to fulfill its fiduciary duty are recruiting, hiring (or firing) and maintaining a solid working relationship with the CEO. A board's best efforts won't go far without the cooperation of a competent executive.

To be most effective, the board needs a CEO who is willing to learn from the board and, in turn, guide it toward understanding both the organization and the health care environment. If the board and CEO respect and trust each other, then together they can set the course for the organization's future. The best boards and CEOs function as a synergistic team, but they should also feel comfortable enough to challenge each other when they disagree or have a different perspective on a problem. The complementary skills and experience of outside directors and the skills and expertise of the health care CEO enhance the likelihood that the organization will continue to be a valuable community asset.

That's why the board-CEO relationship is such a compelling issue for conscientious boards and CEOs, and why we decided to publish this book, a collection of 15 articles previously published in *Trustee* magazine over the past few years. *Better CEO-Board Relations* will take you from start to finish in the typical board-CEO life cycle, from CEO recruitment to executive compensation. In between, you'll find chapters on board-CEO communication and how a CEO's leadership skills affect his or her relationship with the board—in other words, a map of the board-CEO landscape.

The articles were selected with both trustees and CEOs in mind, to help each understand the perspectives and concerns of the other. They offer practical advice—how to interview a CEO candidate, for example—and material designed to broaden trustees' understanding of the CEO's complex role, such as the article "Orchestrating the New Leadership: What It Takes to Be a CEO Today."

Of course, the potential for dissonance and dysfunction is inherent in any relationship, with varying consequences. In a health care organization, negative consequences can be disastrous, and the victims will be patients and the community—the very groups trustees and executives are dedicated to serve. This book is designed to point the board and CEO in the same direction toward success from the start. As the title of an article included in this book suggests, an ideal board-CEO partnership is synergy in motion.

Karen Gardner
Editor, Trustee
Chicago, Illinois

PART ONE

CEO Recruitment

What Kind of CEO Will Your Hospital Need Next? A Model for Succession Planning

By Andrew N. Garman
and J. Larry Tyler

Planning for the incumbent CEO's succession is one of the board's most important responsibilities. Yet for many boards, succession is not discussed until a leadership transition is clearly on the horizon. While deadline-driven agendas serve boards well in many cases, a change of CEO may come up more quickly than expected, so a succession plan should always be in place.

An effective approach to the succession process is to first ask the question, "What kind of leadership will our organization need in the future?" The answer to that question starts with strategy: Where is health care delivery going, and what impact will that direction have on our services and ability to provide them?

When answering these questions, the natural tendency is to think about succession in terms of specific people, rather than skills and talents. But even strong internal candidates will have strengths and limitations, and when "working backward" from the person to the job, the limitations often get overlooked. Knowing what the limitations

---

Andrew N. Garman, Psy.D., is associate professor, Health Systems Management, Rush University Medical Center, Chicago. J. Larry Tyler is president, Tyler & Company, Atlanta.

are, however, can help the board and incoming CEO plan both appropriate development and work design to improve outcomes.

Boards can use a more objective approach by employing a leadership competency model early in the process. Competency models are essentially descriptions of the core capabilities the new CEO needs to have. However, some competencies are easier to articulate than others. For example, we might be able to quickly assess a person's level of knowledge about issuing corporate bonds, but determining a person's ability to "rally the troops" is a much more difficult task. This latter competency is an example of behavioral leadership—that is, the ability to generate enthusiasm among others so that they will be eager to help accomplish a goal that requires a team approach. Behavioral leadership competencies can "make or break" many CEOs' effectiveness and often end up being the hardest for a board to assess.

To help shed some light on these hard-to-define behavioral competencies, we recently conducted a year-long study involving interviews, surveys and validation of a behavioral leadership model. Our first step was to conduct in-depth interviews with 12 executive search consultants specializing in placing senior-level health administrators. Participants represented an even mix of small "boutique" firms and large national or international firms. We asked search consultants to think of individuals who were effective and those who were ineffective in the top management role, and then to describe for us the specific behaviors that contributed to this assessment.

Interview transcripts were analyzed by text analysis software, which allowed us to condense information into competency clusters. Descriptions of the clusters were then circulated to the original survey group and to two new groups of content experts for feedback and validation. The new groups included additional search consultants as well as senior vice presidents of human resources and executive coaches specializing in leadership development. In addition, we asked respondents, based on their personal experience, to determine whether the majority of CEO candidates could master each competency and how many needed development.

This process led to a model of executive leadership with 26 competencies clustered into seven primary dimensions:

- Charting the course
- Inspiring commitment

- Developing work relationships
- Influencing others
- Structuring the work environment
- Communicating
- Self-management

Relationships between these competencies are illustrated in the "Leadership Competency Model," page 6.

The top two boxes in the diagram involve planning and preparation and were deemed by our interviewees to be essential to the CEO position. "Charting the Course" describes the process of strategic planning: analyzing organizational needs and future trends and formulating this analysis into a coherent set of directions for the organization.

One of the quickest ways to determine the "Charting" skill of an executive is to see how he or she responds to questions about the strategic plan. If an executive is not particularly strong on "charting," he or she may have trouble effectively fielding questions about the plan, or may resort to overly vague or emotional justifications rather than facts and logic. Executives who are particularly effective in charting will present strategic plans that are very logical extensions of their environmental analyses.

"Inspiring Commitment" is a complementary dimension, comprising the methods by which a CEO encourages others in the organization to "buy into" a particular strategic direction or plan. For this dimension, the competency deemed most important was building trust. An executive exemplifying this competency is perceived as always being truthful about situations and about himself or herself, someone who can be counted on to follow through on promises and decisions, and someone who often takes the first steps on whatever new path he or she is recommending to a group. Other competencies found to inspire commitment include listening to and receiving feedback, tenacity and professional presence.

In contrast to the first two dimensions, which focus on crafting and getting buy-in for strategic plans, the next three dimensions in the model encompass the tactics used to execute these strategic plans. The "Influencing" dimension relates to a leader's effectiveness in working with people over whom that leader does not have formal or direct administrative authority, such as the medical staff, key members of the community and, of course, board members.

Leadership Competency Model

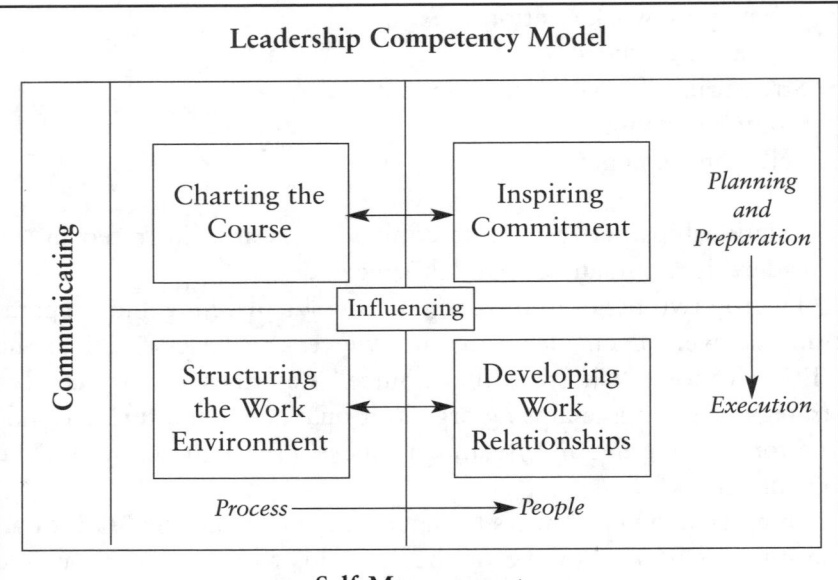

```
Communicating

        Charting the  ←→  Inspiring           Planning
        Course            Commitment          and
                                              Preparation
                  Influencing
                                              ↓
        Structuring  ←→  Developing           Execution
        the Work         Work
        Environment      Relationships

        Process ─────────→ People

Self-Management
```

Competencies in the Model

Charting the Course
- Has strategic vision
- Is innovative
- Thinks in terms of systems
- Is flexible/adaptable

Inspiring Commitment
- Builds trust
- Listens to/solicits feedback
- Is tenacious
- Has a professional presence

Influencing
- Builds consensus
- Is persuasive
- Has political skills
- Fosters collaboration and teamwork

Structuring the Work Environment
- Designs and coordinates work systems
- Gives feedback and guidance on performance and outcomes
- Makes good use of meetings
- Enhances decision making

Developing Work Relationships
- Understands managers' individual values, goals and priorities
- Mentors executives
- Promotes good physician-clinician relations

Communication
- Crafts clear messages
- Energizes staff
- Writes clearly and grammatically
- Speaks well

Self-Management
- Manages personal limitations
- Maintains balance between personal and professional life, practices self-restraint

"Influencing" is a particularly critical dimension in organizations that are politically complex and/or have many political "land mines" (e.g., a merged hospital system in which the premerger organizations had very different missions). Effective influencing requires the ability to rapidly assess stakeholder priorities and goals, combined with skill in using this knowledge to persuade individuals and groups to collaborate on projects and programs. A common example of influencing tactics is the "meeting before the meeting." Executives use this tool to break down barriers ahead of time and ensure a favorable outcome by informing key members of a work group about a decision that will need to be made in an upcoming meeting.

The next two tactical dimensions relate to the more formal administrative structures associated with direct reporting relationships. "Structuring the Work Environment" includes creating robust work systems that deliver accurate information to the right people at the right times. Someone who is effective at structuring the work environment will be able to apply key metrics to information tools (e.g., financial dashboards, patient satisfaction reports) and clearly tie those metrics into ongoing operations, such as regularly scheduled staff meetings, departmental or organizational goal setting and performance appraisals.

The complementary dimension, "Developing Work Relationships," involves understanding management team members' individual values, goals and priorities and then using this knowledge to align managers with opportunities that support the organization while simultaneously facilitating pursuit of their own career goals. Skill in developing work relationships is particularly important when a leader's executive team members are relatively new to their roles, as well as in organizations having difficulty retaining talented executives.

The last two dimensions comprise process skills that can accelerate—or impair—a CEO's effectiveness in each of the other dimensions. "Communicating" is an outwardly focused competency describing the person's abilities to manage and deliver information for maximum impact. Mastery of both methods (oral and written) and style (e.g., articulating goals and priorities for a given audience) was considered essential by the study group. For example, problems in written communications—spelling and grammatical errors in e-mails or memoranda—can quickly call the sender's overall competency level into question.

The final dimension that emerged in the study was "Self-Management," or the CEO's skill in understanding and working effectively around his or her personal limitations (e.g., time, energy, knowledge and skills). Particularly in organizations and environments where the demands on the CEO may be formidable, skills critical for success may include: creative blending of work and home life; recognizing signs of excessive stress; and the ability to marshall additional personal resources (both personal and professional) as necessary.

How a Competency Model Can Inform CEO Selection

A competency model encourages the thoughtful discussions and planning that should take place before beginning the process of considering actual candidates.

Ideally, the process should proceed as follows:

1. The board develops consensus on organizational needs.
2. The board considers the implications of those needs on the organization's current status—e.g., is the hospital poised for expansion? Are there programs or services that need to be restructured or eliminated? To what extent should new collaborative arrangements be developed (e.g., with community colleges or civic groups)? Does the community see the hospital as a provider of quality care?

In thinking through these types of questions, a sense of the necessary CEO competencies will begin to emerge. A strategy that has worked well for us is to interview individual board members and other key stakeholders, using a format structured around the competency model. Results from this process can then be compiled and distilled to prioritize competencies into a coherent profile of the appropriate CEO candidate. With this profile in hand, the board is in a much better position to ensure that succession discussions are driven by organizational needs. Even in cases where the profile does not change the ultimate selection, it can still give the board a more realistic perspective on candidates' strengths and development needs. By addressing these needs early in the selection process, the board and new CEO will be better positioned for success.

Succession Planning: The Art of Transferring Leadership

By Jordan Hadelman
and Elaina Spitaels-Genser

Predicting future trends is the business of futurists. But preparing for predictable circumstances with a clear and decisive plan is the business of all wise and responsible governing bodies. As part of its critical role in selecting and evaluating the CEO, a board must also prepare its organization for the eventual change of executive leadership.

Succession planning helps boards ensure a smooth and orderly transition of leadership. This primer offers trustees a framework on which to build an effective succession plan.

The Case for Succession Planning

The first critical step when developing an effective succession plan is to establish a clear purpose. A board may choose to begin succession planning discussions in order to:

- Groom one or more successors to step into the CEO or other senior leadership roles

---

Jordan Hadelman is chairman and CEO of Witt/Kieffer, Oak Brook, Illinois. Elaina Spitaels-Genser is executive vice president of Witt/Kieffer, Emeryville, California.

- Identify or develop a new leader, internally or externally, pending the CEO's retirement
- Prepare for the unexpected—e.g., the CEO's sudden resignation or dismissal, a serious accident or death
- Decide whether the existing COO, CFO, physician leader or other senior executive—given the opportunity for board exposure, leadership training, job rotation or other professional development—could fill the CEO's shoes
- Assess leadership competencies, skills, experiences and behaviors required of a CEO-in-waiting
- Analyze and modify the current CEO's severance agreement, covering traditional provisions; change-in-control provisions, i.e., when a hospital or health system is acquired or merges with another health organization; and change-in-duties provisions, which seek to define the roles of the departing CEO and/or incoming CEO throughout the transition.

Step One: Establish the Purpose

At the beginning of every succession plan discussion, the board needs to articulate a clear purpose by asking:

- Who wants the plan and why?
- What contingencies need to be addressed? In virtually all cases, the board will want to address what actions should occur when there are vacancies; the strengths and weaknesses of internal leadership; training and development requirements for existing executives; and whether or not to interview executives from the outside.
- What's the timeline for creating the plan? Trustees need to consider which board members, committees, senior managers and other constituencies should provide input on the plan, who will approve it and how much time should be allowed for those processes.
- What's the timeline for finding a successor? For example, perhaps the board wants to prepare for the current CEO's retirement by retaining the COO or other leader and considering him or her for the position. Determining the hiring scenario should help the board determine why it needs a plan, how much time it should allow for the search and what it hopes to gain as a result.
- Who's responsible for drafting the plan? The board may choose to begin succession planning with the full board or it may decide to

assign the job to one of its committees. The key is to keep the process front-and-center on the board's agenda and send the message that succession planning is vital to the organization's future.
- How should the board implement the plan? What are the next steps in grooming and developing leaders in the wings, or assessing critical competencies?
- How and when should key staff be informed about the plan?

Step Two: Review Strategic Goals

As part of the initial succession planning discussion, the board needs to ask itself these questions:

- What is the organization's vision of the future?
- What are the organization's leadership requirements—both short-term and long-term—to achieve the vision?
- What are its strategic goals?
- Where are the gaps in existing leadership competencies?

Step Three: Initiate CEO Succession Planning

Traditionally, the topic of succession planning has been difficult for hospital boards to broach, causing health care to lag behind public companies in formalizing these plans. If the board raises the topic of succession planning, the CEO may feel as if he or she is being eased out. Conversely, if the CEO brings up the topic, the board may wonder if the chief executive is preparing to leave.

A good starting point is the CEO's annual performance evaluation, which should include a discussion of his or her professional and personal goals, future aspirations and job satisfaction. The evaluation should also address how well the CEO performs and fits in his or her current position and discuss developmental needs, leadership style, values, skills and behaviors.

At the same time, trustees should consider the age and tenure of their CEO. An older CEO may be considering, at a minimum, a lifestyle change that reduces time on the job or possibly, full retirement. Younger CEOs may be eager to see career progression, either in their current role or elsewhere, whereas CEOs with school-age or college-bound children may be seeking stability in a longer-term contract.

Five Key Components

Most CEO succession plans have at least five elements in common:

1. An action plan that details what must be done and who should be in charge of making it happen.
2. A succession profile that outlines competencies and requirements for the new CEO.
3. A communications plan describing how the plan will be announced to specific internal and external audiences.
4. Opportunities for physician leaders to provide the medical staff's perspective on CEO succession.
5. A compensation discussion that outlines how both the retiring and future CEO will be rewarded for successfully implementing the succession plan. For example, an incoming CEO may be provided incentives by the board to hold off making immediate changes in key executive positions until mutually agreed upon timeframes for change are determined. The board may want to consider compensation incentives that create "golden handcuffs" to retain top talent. If they decide to do so, the board must be aware of current market trends and regulatory requirements of CEO compensation. The board may also retain a retiring CEO as a consultant so that he or she can become fully vested in the retirement plan. Trustees may also want to consider other financial retention strategies, such as supplemental executive retirement plans (SERP) fashioned to include long-term incentive payouts.

The Three Basic Plans

Health care boards should focus on developing succession plans that address three primary causes of CEO departure. Each plan outlines the specific actions the board would take in the event of a planned or unplanned leadership vacancy.

1. **Unexpected Emergency Plan**

    This is the succession planning strategy an organization needs if its CEO becomes incapacitated or dies. It is essential that all health care organizations have a documented emergency plan in place. A useful outline should look something like the following:

A. Actions Required
   a. Identify someone in the organization who can assume the role of interim CEO. Ask senior managers and physician executives for their opinion, and listen to whose name is mentioned most often.
   b. Draft a board resolution that appoints the interim CEO. All members of the senior management team will report to this designated individual during the interim period.

A Compression of Talent

Over the past two decades, health care organizations have experienced a "compression" of executive talent, meaning that more must be done with fewer potential leaders. In prior years, hospitals and health systems were structured with multiple layers of management, and it wasn't uncommon to have assistant vice presidents and directors in each functional area.

This changed radically once managed care redefined the delivery and business of health care. Organizations were stripped of managers and executives waiting in the wings. The result: a dwindling pool of future leaders, leaving many health care organizations with a dearth of qualified internal candidates.

Compounding the problem is the looming age of baby boomers and a probable shortfall of young executives ready to step into CEO roles. Over the next decade, replacing aging CEOs will be the board's biggest challenge. Baby boomers who reach age 65 by 2011 will retire in large numbers.

Similarly, younger boomers will reevaluate their work/life commitments and may choose to leave the "pressure cooker" health care environment even sooner. The combined effect could create a significant executive leadership void.

Meanwhile, professional recruiters report a scarcity in the number of qualified young executives being groomed to become CEOs. Recruiters also note that the rising Generation X seems more selective than their predecessors when considering a new position. Many hesitate to accept new posts unless they consider the job a perfect fit. The likely gap between capable future leaders and open CEO spots will create a scenario decidedly in favor of talented younger executives.

      c. Make appropriate arrangements with banks and other entities granting the interim CEO signing authority.
  B. Contingency Plans
      a. If the CEO is incapacitated, how long will recovery take? What will happen in the interim? If the vacancy is permanent, what happens next?
      b. Should the interim CEO be appointed permanently, or is a search necessary?
      c. Does the board want to conduct an internal or external search? Does it want to retain a search firm in the event of an external search?
  C. Crisis Communications
      a. Have a crisis communication plan ready for immediate implementation.
      b. Designate an official spokesperson to lead press conferences and handle all external inquiries.
      c. Develop an internal communication plan and update staff regularly.

2. **Transitional Plan**

A transition plan is implemented in the event a CEO resigns to take another position or is asked to leave. Unlike the unexpected/emergency succession plan, the board has more time to consider the direction it wants to take. The important issues the board needs to address are to:

  A. Define the Timeframe
      a. Does the CEO's contract stipulate how much notice must be given? This will help the board decide whether it will need to appoint or hire an interim CEO. However, a board may choose not to honor the stipulation because holding a departing CEO to his or her contract may create a "lame-duck" scenario that stalls momentum in finding a replacement.
      b. How long will it take to conduct a search, if needed, for the new CEO?
  B. Identify Knowledge, Experience, Competencies
      The success profile of the new CEO comprises essential knowledge, prior experience, leadership competencies and behavior

strengths and drives what an organization seeks in a new executive. When drafting a profile, trustees should be as specific as possible when defining competencies, such as being a team builder, being politically savvy, having the right customer focus and good interpersonal skills, being visionary, results-oriented, composed and able to inspire confidence.

C. Evaluate Internal Candidates

Is there an existing executive who has the leadership requirements needed to achieve the organization's vision and goals? Even if the answer is yes, the board may choose to conduct an external search to compare its internal choice for CEO with external candidates. This often enhances the credibility of the internal candidate in assuming the new role.

3. Anticipatory Plan

Although similar to transitional planning, this succession plan should be developed when a CEO indicates he or she is planning to retire.

A. Define the Timeframe

Ideally, CEOs should inform the board of their decision 18 to 24 months prior to their retirement date. If there's a designated management team member who will assume the CEO role, this provides time for the board to get to know him or her before that person steps into the new job.

B. Choose Either a "CEO-in-Training" or an Experienced Leader

One familiar scenario is the CEO who has been in the position 25 or more years and gives the board ample notice of his or her pending retirement. The age of the management team is often similar to that of the retiring CEO, so the board elects to launch an external search prior to the current CEO's departure. Or the board may consider searching for an heir apparent immediately—an executive vice president, for example, who comes in and learns the organization under the current CEO.

C. Pave the Way for New Leadership

If the retiring CEO's reputation has assumed heroic proportions, which is often the case if he or she has been with the organization for many years, a newly appointed CEO with a radically different leadership style may create unease among a variety of constituents. Often, however, a change in leadership direction is both vital and necessary in order to achieve organizational goals. That means the board must determine how to pave the way—with management, employees, physicians and the community—for the new CEO's success.

Succession Plans in Action: Two Case Studies

Succession plans are like fingerprints—no two are alike, and they leave an impression on everything they touch. How a board approaches succession planning leaves its mark on the future success of its organization.

Following are real-life examples of how two very different health care organizations—one with a succession plan and one without—approached this crucial governance responsibility.

A Model Approach
For more than 10 years, this urban East Coast–based health system (called "System A" here), comprising five hospitals and covering a broad service population of 350,000, has had an extensive history of leadership development, actively promoting needed development for all its executive staff.

As a result, the system has a full pipeline of internal leaders and a succession plan that asks senior managers to:

- Conduct performance reviews that encourage open discussion between managers, discussing their career goals and how they can develop them.
- Incorporate 360-degree analyses into performance reviews/evaluations and provide other opportunities for executive assessment.

Performance reviews serve as a valuable tool in leadership assessment and development.

The process involves an active exchange of ideas and emphasizes each individual executive's personal career goals and long-term aspirations.

Continued →

Such an evaluation also offers developmental opportunities and honest analysis and feedback of the executive's strengths and weaknesses.

- Encourage job rotation within the system.

Because hospital operations are contained within a geographic region, System A can offer executive job rotation opportunities among its various member hospitals. Such rotation permits career growth without personal and/or family upheaval.

Nevertheless, losing talented staff is inevitable. But what distinguishes this system is how it plans for such losses. Attrition is incorporated into succession planning.

To balance the anticipated loss, the board and CEO have been committed to finding potential new leaders within the system. To date, they have identified more than 75 potential executives.

The board has also made the wise decision to involve its medical staff in succession planning. Previously, only the chief of staff had direct contact with the board.

An underlying benefit to greater medical staff involvement is that the board's actions convey to the medical staff that their opinions and ideas are valued.

A Lack of Foresight
"Hospital B," a 300-bed teaching hospital located in a Midwestern suburban location, does not have a formal plan for leadership development. Developing a formal succession plan and leadership development program rests with the board and CEO.

Although Hospital B has encouraged mentoring for its senior management team, it has been implemented by only a few, and no one has been accountable for identifying and grooming potential leaders. This lack of foresight and planning has left the organization unprepared to replace key executives when they resign.

So, when the board chair stepped down, followed closely by the CEO's announced plan to retire—each of whom had held their positions for more than 25 years—the board was unprepared to deal with the impending dual loss, and the organization was thrown into confusion.

Continued →

> **Lessons Learned**
>
> Unwittingly, the board had exacerbated the problem by communicating only with the CEO, effectively excluding senior management and the medical staff from contributing to top-level decisions. This produced an atmosphere of secrecy and suspicion, which led talented staff to seek career opportunities elsewhere.
>
> As a result of this confusion and a destructive leadership culture, it has taken longer than anticipated to replace both executives. The CEO is still on the job without a replacement in the wings.
>
> After nine months of lost time, Hospital B has now retained an executive search firm.
>
> The board realized that its failure to discuss succession planning cost Hospital B valuable time, so trustees reviewed what happened and identified ways to better prepare for the future.
>
> They have decided to:
> - Engage the board and CEO in regular succession planning discussions.
> - Fill board vacancies quickly.
> - Determine ways in which the board can have more exposure to other leaders in the organization and invest in leadership development for physicians and others.
> - Engage physician leaders to develop leadership training programs for appropriate members of the medical staff.
> - Seek outside help earlier in the leadership transition process. After nine months of lost time, Hospital B has now retained an executive search firm.

The Next Generation

The more qualified candidates an organization has, the stronger the organization. Limiting the slate of potential leaders, particularly to the CEO's direct reports, puts the board in a bind. Not all direct reports will step naturally into senior roles. Those chosen to be retained, however, should be reassured their positions are secure even if they fail to make the CEO cut.

Establish a "pipeline" of executives with high leadership potential by offering them education: e.g., management skills training, job cross-training, job rotation and opportunities to interact with the board and medical staff. Best practices in leadership development also include offering off-site retreats, executive critique sessions, 360-degree feedback and leadership academy enrollment.

Succession Planning Reminders

Succession planning is a journey—not a destination. There are, however, important sign posts along the road:

- Keep it strategic. A succession plan supports an organization's strategic goals. What an organization cultivates in existing leaders—and looks for in new executives—depends on its future plans.
- Stay in the driver's seat. Succession planning is the board's duty, but the CEO must ride shotgun. Meanwhile, the CEO is responsible for succession planning and leadership development among the rest of the management team.
- Put it in writing. Having a written document provides a road map and a record of the board's deliberations, protecting it if the CEO or board chair were to leave unexpectedly.
- Keep the engine tuned. A succession plan is not something that, once complete, is put to the side. At a minimum, the board should revisit the plan annually, preferably semiannually.
- Tell those who need to know. Making the succession plan too widely known too early can produce a "lame-duck" scenario for your current CEO. On the other hand, limiting knowledge of the plan to a select few—such as the board's executive committee—can create an awkward situation for executives and physician leaders left in the dark.
- Track your progress. Too often boards draft a plan and then fail to review it, act on it and/or measure their progress. Then, when something unexpected happens, the board discovers the plan is dated or of little value, or the organization is left with a promising leader who is still not yet ready to assume the CEO role.

The Art of Interviewing Your Next CEO

By David W. Thompson
and Nancie Noie Thompson

Ineffective management is one of the costliest, most disruptive problems for an organization. Yet the procedure for selecting chief executives is ambiguous at best. Too often the process is ill-defined and the responsibility diffuse—when everyone has responsibility, no one is held accountable.

Boards of sophisticated organizations have long recognized that the best employees do not necessarily make the best managers. They know that each position has its own demands and its own milieu. Indeed, they also know that one organization's star CEO is not necessarily another's.

So it follows that the board's first task should be to define what type of an executive would be most effective for that time and place. If, for example, an organization has grown "fat" because the previous CEO lost control of the budget, the new CEO should be someone

---

David W. Thompson, Ph.D., is a management consulting psychologist in Chicago. Nancie Noie Thompson is executive director of the Alliance of Independent Academic Medical Centers, Chicago, and president of Nancie Noie & Associates, Chicago.

who is very efficient, authoritative and has the confidence to motivate managers to lay off non-essential personnel.

The most effective selection processes evaluate an individual's personality characteristics and match them to the characteristics needed in a given position. Why personality characteristics? Because studies show that it is these characteristics that account for more than 90 percent of failures in any given position.

Too often boards select CEOs on the basis of past performance; however, this is a mistake because:

- Past performance is difficult to interpret objectively, especially at the CEO level.
- Performance results are the consequence of numerous variables, many of which cannot be controlled.
- Any selection/promotion means moving a person into a new environment where he/she will confront different demands, problems, expectations, personalities and responsibilities—e.g., some highly effective chief operating officers are not nearly as effective in a CEO position.

Promotion and hiring decisions should be based on the governing board's best prediction of how the person will function in the new position, and that prediction will be most reliable when it's based on the only available data it has—the candidate's behavior.

One of the best methods of observing behavior is the interview—but not the interview of the past. The interview gives the board a dual opportunity: first, to observe the candidate's behavior; and second, to interpret his or her behavior. Since our ultimate goal is to know who the individual truly is, let's turn first to interpretation.

Content versus Behavioral Interpretations

There are two ways to interpret another person's behavior. One is the way we have been taught all our lives. This is content interpretation—focusing on what the person is saying. The other way is to focus on what the person's behavior is telling us. This is behavioral interpretation. For example:

Interviewee: "I went to Greece last year, and it was beautiful! The islands were peaceful, really inspiring. The water was unbelievably clear. It was one of the best vacations I ever had!"

Trustee interviewer's content interpretation: "Maybe I should consider Greece for my next vacation." Here we are not thinking of the person doing the talking, just the thing they are talking about (i.e., Greece). This is the way we have been taught to think and the way we should think most of the time.

Behavioral interpretation: "This person is positive and enthusiastic." How does the trustee know this? He or she just observed that behavior. Here the interviewer heard what the prospective CEO said only insofar as it told him or her something about that person. The candidate could just as easily have been talking about widgets, dogs or stairs. But we can only judge people fairly in terms of their repetitive behavior—one response tells us little. So they must speak enthusiastically at least three times during the interview before the interviewers can arrive sensibly at this conclusion.

Interviewee: "I went to Athens last year. It was awful! The air was filthy, the people were surly and getting around by car was impossible because the people are such terrible drivers."

Trustee interviewer's content interpretation: "I should be hesitant about going to Athens on my next vacation."

Behavioral interpretation: "This person is negative and overly critical." If this type of behavior occurs repeatedly during the interview and the board hires him or her, the people with whom this individual interacts will be frequently subjected to negative attitudes.

Frequently, content and behavioral interpretations conflict, so it's wise to evaluate the candidate on behavior. A few examples:

In an interview the candidate says, "Giving speeches always makes me nervous." Is this person revealing a lack of confidence? A content interpretation would lead one to conclude that the candidate is not confident; after all, he just told us he gets nervous. A behavioral interpretation tells us just the opposite, however—i.e., telling someone he gets nervous is a very confident response because he is strong enough to be honest about a personality trait that might be perceived as negative.

Making the Switch

Choosing to make a behavioral interpretation over a content interpretation can be difficult, but it is essential. It's the person's behavior that will have the greatest impact on the organization and the people in it. This is especially true in the case of a CEO, whose behavior will affect and influence the whole organization.

If trustees ask interviewees to describe a previous position, they have no way of knowing whether the description is accurate, nor should they care. They do know, however, what the interviewees emphasize in their description, and this is what leads to a meaningful interpretation.

People can easily change the content (and always do) of what they say to others. It is very difficult, however, to change who they are. It is difficult for a person with a strong need for precision (possibly a micromanager) not to be precise and detailed in the interview: "I was with that hospital 14 months; no, actually it was a little over 14, closer to 15 months." This is not to suggest that a micromanager will necessarily be ineffective; again, it depends on the needs of the organization at that time.

Suppose trustees ask CEO candidates to describe the culture of a hospital in which they worked 10 years ago. We don't know if their descriptions are accurate, nor is this important. We can listen to what they are emphasizing, however, and their behavior when they are describing the hospital's culture. Their answers (which may be well-organized, overly negative or reflect indecisiveness) may reveal a great deal about themselves. Hypercritical candidates, for example, have difficulty controlling their tendencies to criticize when they are discussing situations aversive to them, and this tendency is a relevant factor in the selection decision.

When the board is swayed by content, not behavior, it often results in the best "salesperson" getting the job, because he or she is adept at using persuasive content.

Five Principles for Encouraging Sincere, Spontaneous Behavior

The goal of asking questions is to be able to make accurate and insightful interpretations. But those insights will depend entirely on the interviewers' ability to draw out another person's spontaneous and true behavior. The inability to understand/interpret behavior accurately is almost always a result of an inability to do a good job of bringing out spontaneous behavior from the other person. Here are some guidelines for doing this:

1. Don't be judgmental. A nonjudgmental attitude is critical to a successful evaluation. No matter what interviewers feel, they should keep their views to themselves—they're not trying to influence candidates, they're trying to evaluate them. When interviewers are judgmental, they make their candidates uneasy and concerned over reactions to their opinions. As a result, they may start to behave insincerely.

If, for example, a trustee interviewer reveals, even subtly, that he or she doesn't like people who are hypercritical, candidates may guard that behavior in themselves. But being negative and critical may be their true nature. If they are ultimately hired, that negative attitude will eventually surface and could have a destructive influence on the organization.

2. Ask broad, general questions. This allows people to focus on what's interesting and important to them. These are the issues with which they feel safe. Broad, general questions are non-threatening; hence they elicit spontaneity.

Whoever asks the questions controls the interaction. Since asking questions gives us so much control, we tend to ask too many in areas that reflect our own interests. Bringing forth a person's typical behavior requires that we give him or her ostensible control in picking the topic. Our questions, consequently, should allow the person as much leeway as possible in responding. So we should ask broad, general questions that are somewhat ambiguous and allow the other person to respond in any way he or she wishes. Some examples of good and bad questions:

Bad: "How long have you known Bill?"
Good: "What's Bill like?"

Bad: "When did you leave St. Louis?"
Good: "How was St. Louis?"

Bad: "Who runs the department?"
Good: "How's the department run?"

Bad: "When did you move to New York?"
Good: "How did you feel about moving to New York?"

Give candidates freedom to be spontaneous. It's not the right time to force them to focus on what interviewers are interested in so that they don't get bored, nor is it the right time to try to impress candidates.

Trustees and directors often feel more comfortable with narrow, factual questions that leave little to chance. Such questions are not appropriate in an interview. Some examples of responses to narrow, factual versus broad, general questions:

> "I've headed up the department three years" tells us little. "The department has a lot of problems, such as . . ." can tell us a great deal.
>
> "I met Bill at a party" doesn't tell us much. "What I like about Bill is his thoughtfulness. He's one of the most considerate . . ." can tell us a lot.
>
> "I started flying when I came out of the Navy" is of little real consequence. "I love the freedom of flying, of being away from anyone telling me what I should or shouldn't do . . ." tells us a great deal.
>
> "I moved here six months ago" can lead everyone (including the speaker) to yawn in boredom. "I like it here because the people seem so friendly and outgoing. I've probably made more friends . . ." opens up the possibility of relevant interpretations.

Allowing candidates to discuss whatever they like not only encourages sincerity but also tells us two important things: what they feel most comfortable talking about, and where they focus their energy.

3. Ask probing questions. Most people will respond initially to general questions in a perfunctory way. "What kind of person was the COO?" will often elicit, for example, a quick answer such as, "She was fine."

This happens because most people have learned that interviewers are not genuinely interested in their views at all. Consider the following typical exchange:

> **Interviewer 1:** "How do you like your apartment?" (Good question)
> **Interviewee:** "I like it a lot."
> **Interviewer 1:** "Actually, I once looked at apartments in that building." (Bad Response)
> **Interviewer 2:** "I remember an apartment I once had in Sacramento. It. . . ." (Worse)

Interviewer 3: "I used to think renting was the way to go, but after doing a careful analysis, I concluded. . . ." (Terrible)

It may be a shock to interviewees when they are confronted by probing questions to their perfunctory answers, such as "How so?" "Because?" "In the sense of?" As you can see, a probe is a short, quick, follow-up question that asks the person for more. A probe tells people that we're interested in them.

Probing often alleviates candidates' fear of being seen as boring, insignificant or unimportant. It encourages confidence and, hence, open, spontaneous behavior that is typical of the person.

No behavior will tell you more about a person than the behavior you draw out by probing. Why? Because you're asking interviewees to elaborate on their feelings, attitudes and concerns. And you're not asking them to do so in order to argue with them or belittle them. You're not being judgmental. So the only reason you could be probing is because you're really interested in what they're saying. And with such a respectful, receptive audience, people will be more likely to be open and honest.

Interviewer: "How is Bill as a person?"
Interviewee: "Good."
Interviewer: "How so?"

Interviewee: "The people who run our accounting department really do a lousy job!"
Interviewer: "How so?" (Instead of "That's nothing; you should see ours. You wouldn't believe what we have to put up with. Why, just the other day. . . .")

Interviewee: "I think I need a change of scenery."
Interviewer: "Because?" (Instead of "You and me both.")

Interviewee: "I like a small-town atmosphere."
Interviewer: "Because?" (Instead of "You're kidding. I'd be bored to death.")

Probing is difficult because listening to someone else often leads to an overwhelming desire to influence, to change the other person's views and to get him or her to focus on, and be impressed by, us. (After all, we may well have been chosen to be a trustee because we're judgmental, authoritative and controlling.)

4. Use a soft, gentle, inflected tone of voice. This encourages people to feel comfortable and spontaneous rather than threatened. A gentle, inflected tone shows respect and further alleviates the fear of being challenged, dominated, insulted or involved in a competition with the interviewers.

Commanding: "Tell me about your department."
Soft, gentle, inflected: "Would you tell me a little about your department?"

Commanding: "Why don't you tell me about yourself!"
Soft, inflected, interested and respectful: "Would you please tell me a little about yourself?"

A low, flat, authoritative tone of voice generally makes the other person guarded, defensive and resentful. It encourages atypical behavior. The gentle, inflected, respectful approach generally makes the other person comfortable, spontaneous, relaxed, happy and open. It will put the person at ease. And that's what you want, because then they're more likely to be themselves.

5. Let candidates lead the way. Whenever possible, base questions on some part of the interviewee's last response. In doing so, trustees send the message that they are truly listening and want to discuss the things that the candidate wants to discuss. Because trustees are following the interviewee's lead, they alleviate his or her fear of being controlled.

Suppose board members are talking to a prospective candidate who recently moved to Chicago from St. Louis and just mentioned that fact. Good questions might be "How was St. Louis?" or "How do you like Chicago?" or "How would you compare Chicago to St. Louis?" (Then follow their potentially perfunctory response with a probe.)

Bad follow-up questions would be "Do you agree with the AHA policy on medical ethics?" or "What years were you in college?" or "How long did it take you to finish your MBA?" These "non sequiturs" tell the person we really don't care about him, that we have our own agenda to which he must subscribe.

Summary

If conducted properly, an interview is a highly effective tool for evaluating managers at any level of an organization. Broad, general questions, gently put, elicit sincere behavior from others, allowing them the freedom to respond as they wish. Their responses tell us what they typically focus on. Moreover, the interviewee is inclined to find us "safe" to talk to. This reduces his or her fear or discomfort, which should be any interviewer's goal.

Probing often elicits the most spontaneous, hence truest, behavior revealing who this person is and how he or she will respond in a particular position or situation. Good probes, which should be used frequently in any conversation, also convey the message that we care about the interviewee and his or her views.

Interviewing means focusing on others. It should be an integral part of the board's repertoire of skills. It is also an integral part of being a good manager. Few people are emotionally capable of implementing the principles described here. It is incumbent on the board, therefore, to select those members who can conduct in-depth interviews for a new CEO.

Managing CEO Transition

By John R. Gardner

CEO turnover has become all too common in hospitals. The American College of Healthcare Executives reported that the turnover rate for hospital CEOs in 2004 was 16 percent, which means that almost every week, more than a dozen hospital boards are challenged to replace their leadership.

When faced with CEO turnover, the hospital board must have a plan to fill the leadership gap on an interim basis.

The position could be filled through an outside firm that maintains a pool of experienced hospital executives available for short-term interim assignments, or the board may appoint a member of the hospital's leadership team to serve as the interim CEO. The effectiveness of the interim CEO sets the stage for the arrival of the new CEO. When an interim management plan is successful, the organization can move forward, building from existing momentum. But mismanaged

---

John R. Gardner is currently an interim administrator with Grand River Hospital District in Rifle, Colorado. The author acknowledges the support of Jaren Wilson, a consultant with Denver-based Policy Studies Inc., who provided research for this article.

interim leadership sets the stage for lost ground that will have to be restored and may never be recovered by the new CEO.

The CEO's departure may create harmful organizational dynamics. As the CEO prepares to leave, the remaining members of the leadership team are likely to experience anxiety and uncertainty. These feelings can permeate the entire organization, leading to defections of valued employees and medical staff. These losses damage the hospital's ability to function optimally.

During this period, the board may decide to designate an interim CEO. Whether the board opts to appoint an internal transitional leader or bring in an outside executive to fill the role, it must set the stage for the interim CEO to lead the hospital effectively.

Key Guidance from the Board to the Interim CEO

When the board appoints an interim CEO, it needs to establish performance expectations that extend beyond the usual financial performance and quality-of-care standards. The following guidelines should be given to the interim CEO to clarify his or her role during the search for a permanent CEO:

1. Avoid a "minding the shop" mentality. Executive searches frequently take considerably longer than anticipated. Choosing a "holding pattern" during this time (usually from six to nine months), with no focus on strategy or operations, can result in a significant and costly setback for the hospital.

    The interim CEO must behave as if he or she has the permanent role. Decisions that help the hospital grow and thrive should not be put on hold until the permanent CEO arrives. Credibility must be maintained with the hospital's internal and external stakeholders, and business priorities must be articulated.
2. Focus on the executive team and its needs. If the interim CEO is going to succeed, he or she must create an environment of trust and open communication by sharing the board's expectations of the leadership team. As decisions are made, consult with the leadership team and encourage input. When this doesn't happen, the hospital is rudderless.
3. Define a shared situational understanding. Interim CEOs will be hard-pressed to succeed if their understanding of organizational conditions and challenges is different from others on the executive team. Interim CEOs will receive a tremendous amount of

information about the organization in a short amount of time. As they learn about the culture of the hospital, its financial condition, the local market, medical staff issues, etc., a picture of what challenges the hospital may be facing and how to face them will begin to form.

Interim CEOs must share their perceptions with the executive team and reach agreement on how problems are defined, what strategies to use for addressing them and the assignment of responsibility. Without this shared understanding, it is difficult, if not impossible, to achieve cooperation or agreement on the organization's priorities.

4. Focus on strategy. Without a focus on strategy, hospital leaders remaining with the hospital will tend to fix their attention on their future role (if there is to be one) in the organization. Until the leadership team is aligned with organizational expectations and priorities, the hospital may be on a path to failure.

   To avoid this pitfall, the interim leader must assemble the leadership team to identify and discuss the priorities of the hospital. A focus on strategy will help guide the team through such difficult issues as poor financial performance, medical staff challenges or competitor strategies.

5. Communicate, communicate, communicate. The interim CEO needs to communicate with all the various stakeholders of the hospital. Frequent communication with employees, physicians, board members and sponsoring organizations is vital. Communication should focus on what has been accomplished, decisions that have been made and, where appropriate, the challenges that the organization is facing. The absence of communication creates an opportunity for rumors as stakeholders begin to speculate on what is happening in the organization.

   Two examples of effective communication are: weekly communication to the board of directors, employees and medical staff describing key events, hospital utilization, financial performance and critical challenges the hospital is facing; and meeting with the local media to apprise them of the state of the hospital.

The hospital board's leadership during a CEO transition sets the stage for the successor and the future of the hospital. The above guidelines provide a foundation for communicating leadership expectations and accountability to the interim CEO and the management team.

PART TWO

∞

Communication

Behind Closed Doors: Should the Board Hold Executive Sessions?

By Laurie Larson

Whispering is usually considered rude in a group, because whoever can't hear what's being said usually feels that the discussion must be about him or her and that it must be negative. The same might be said of how CEOs and other staff members who regularly attend board meetings (e.g., the CFO, CIO) might feel about executive session—that is, when the board meets privately without them.

At a recent meeting of the American Hospital Association's Committee on Governance (COG), a strongly opinionated and divided discussion developed around when or if the board should meet in executive session beyond annual discussions of the CEO's compensation and performance and, increasingly, the audit. Following is an elaboration of that discussion, along with some outside points of view.

COG member Doug Wall, vice chair of University Medical Center at the University of Arizona, Tucson, is firmly opposed to the practice.

"I've served on many [types of] boards and my experience tells me that [there] has to be a partnership, a team approach, between

---

Laurie Larson is *Trustee*'s associate editor.

the board and the CEO," Wall says. "That's the driving force in every successful company."

Wall believes that if the board decides to meet without the CEO beyond his or her annual compensation and performance review, it can only mean that there are "serious issues around the CEO," such as charges of sexual harassment, hiding information from the board and the like.

"Absent that, 99 percent of the time the CEO is trying to run an organization he is proud of. [To] have meetings with only the board runs against the grain for the morale of the whole organization," Wall says. "There's no CEO alive who won't feel threatened and worried. . . . I can't tell you how undermining it is to an administrator if they don't feel they have 100 percent board trust and support. It will affect every decision [he or she] makes."

"Serious issues," i.e., those potentially related to some crime or inappropriate behavior by the CEO, need to be discerned from "sensitive issues," Wall says, which are those discussions or issues about which the board may have strongly divided opinions and prefer to avoid discussing.

"Any issue where the CEO is going off in one direction and the board in another should be put on the table for all to discuss. . . . Everyone has to deal with it, iron it out together," Wall says. He believes that if there is a lack of trust, which executive sessions tend to imply, it's time for the board to either seek a new CEO or immediately review its own conduct. If it does the latter, trustees should ask themselves if they are involving themselves too deeply in administrative or operational activities. "It's the nature of many board members to want to delve into how the hospital runs—anything from parking to patient experience," Wall says. "Trustees would like to substitute their judgment for the CEO's."

Other COG members, however, such as Richard Haeder, a trustee from Rapid City (S.D.) Regional Hospital, think the current regulatory times demand more of that exact kind of action from trustees.

"There is a thrust by government at all levels to make sure that board members do more and have more independent judgment on what the hospital's business is. Directors will be held responsible," Haeder says. "The Sarbanes-Oxley laws used in the private sector will eventually be applied [to not-for-profit boards]. It's better legal protection to have executive sessions." Haeder explains, "There is an element of management in everything a director does. Active management by the CEO and active governance go together; they're not a contradiction."

COG member Rulon Stacey agrees with him—but only to a point. "It's unrealistic to expect that the board will not meet without the CEO," says Stacey, CEO of Poudre Valley Hospital, Fort Collins, Colorado. "A good board will evaluate the CEO every year on performance and salary without him being present—it's prudent." It is similarly prudent, particularly in the wake of scandals like Enron, he says, for the finance committee (or the full board) to meet alone with the auditors—in fact, he thinks the CEO should insist that he or she be excluded from the audit meeting.

Having said that much, however, Stacey states firmly, "A board that has executive sessions all the time is a dysfunctional board. There is no scenario where the CEO should be excused every meeting. He or she misses out on the opportunity to direct the organization. If you don't feel like you can talk about strategy or operations or other things with the CEO there, you need to get another CEO."

Make It Standard Policy

Haeder counters that the sting and intimidation associated with executive session can be avoided by writing an official policy into the board's bylaws on when an executive session should be called, thereby standardizing the use of such sessions. He thinks executive sessions should be called four times a year at a minimum, with every other month preferred. He emphasizes that an executive session is not, and should not be, used for micromanaging, but to give board members the opportunity to ask broader-ranging questions.

"The reason you sit on the board is to bring the layman's opinion and viewpoint. Boards that can get together in a free-form discussion can bring up more topics," Haeder says. "It better allows the directors to marshall the company, ask questions and feed off of each other. It allows the developing situation to inform the conversation . . . and it encourages participation, not just [passive] listening."

Larry Walker, president of The Walker Company, a health care management and governance consulting firm in Lake Oswego, Oregon, agrees with Haeder, explaining that if executive session is part of board policy, "it removes the natural anxiety the CEO or other staff members might feel [in being excluded]."

He thinks that calling an executive session unexpectedly creates the perception of secrecy. "When an executive session is [suddenly] called, it causes rumors and unnecessary hand-wringing," Walker says. A standing policy and procedure is critical to avoid such perceptions, he believes—with no surprises.

"If there is some new problem that has just come up, executive session can be a way to stay ahead of the rumor mill," Walker says. "The more something needs to be kept confidential, where liability or reputation is involved, [that's the time for] executive session."

However, he adds that executive session is not appropriate "as an excuse to create an issue where one doesn't exist" or to address problems that are management issues. "You don't want to use executive session to raise issues that ought to be discussed in a full board meeting," Walker says. And he adds, "Only the board chair should decide when or if to call executive session as a part of board policy. It shouldn't be called for reasons not explained or justified and it shouldn't be used to duck legitimate board discussion, even if it's uncomfortable. Executive session can be a way to hide from difficult discussions."

Or to talk too much about the wrong things, in COG member John Smallmon's experience. Smallmon is chair of the Good Shepherd Health Care System in Hermiston, Oregon, and he has seen executive sessions backfire.

Two years ago, some members of Smallmon's hospital's medical staff had complaints about the administration. The current board chair decided to have an executive session to discuss their problems and the rumors that had been circulating. Before the session, some trustees spoke to medical staff members directly, but they were not included in the session. Smallmon says the session sparked rumors that the CEO was leaving, so to counter that buzz, the board moved to have 10 to 15 minutes at the end of every subsequent board meeting reserved for executive session to make it more "routine."

Subsequently, Smallmon says, there were a few board members who had to be reminded constantly not to get into operational discussions during the sessions, and, after six months, he and some other trustees told the chair that it wasn't working. The board then went on a retreat, led by a consultant, during which trustees agreed that they were using executive sessions inappropriately and needed to better target their actions.

"We formed a physicians' relations committee with board members and [concerned] medical staff, with the blessing of the CEO," Smallmon explains. "The doctors felt the CEO was hiding information from them, and we were able to assure them that this was not the case and that the board and CEO were of one mind. It was a better solution to the same problem than a general executive session—and it didn't build [staff] division this way." Smallmon says they were able to explain the physicians' basic complaints to the CEO and the board's response to those complaints without getting into details, and relations have improved greatly since.

How to Set Policy

"The board (including the CEO) should have an open discussion on executive session policy and what its uses, advantages and disadvantages might be," Walker advises. Alternatively, a board subcommittee could be formed to discuss the executive session policy's full shape.

He says executive session policy should have: a title; an articulated purpose(s); the date it was created and a designated time for reviewing and possibly amending it; an explanation of the process for calling it and who may do so; and a determination as to whether it will be a standard agenda item or whether it will be voted on at each meeting. The policy should also discuss what kinds of written records should be kept and who should see them.

Trustees should look at how they currently use executive session, as well as their existing committee structure to see if workable meeting processes already exist; for example, the executive committee may be able to cover many topics as effectively as an executive session.

Good reasons for executive sessions might include gathering information relative to allegations of patient abuse or fraud, real estate acquisition, potential litigation or merger discussions.

Walker adds that such specific examples should be included in the policy to help define when and why the session would be called. And although the session implies by its nature that the CEO be absent, even that does not have to be a hard-and-fast rule. In fact, he believes that CEOs should always be in an executive session unless it concerns his or her compensation or evaluation.

"The board should be free to invite the CEO or others to executive session—the key is that the discussion be completely confidential, not a part of the [regular] board meeting or minutes, that the minutes are available only to the board—that what happens in the session stays there," Walker says. Those who should be excluded from executive session certainly would include the public (in the case of a public hospital), managers, chiefs of staff, attorneys—"those who don't have decision-making authority," Walker summarizes.

He also recommends that any executive session be limited to only one topic—"otherwise you have a shadow agenda," a meeting under the radar of the regular board meeting. Overall, he believes that the calling of an executive session must always be weighed against perceptions of secrecy. "It [the executive session] should not be ad hoc, not anecdotal, not a free-for-all," he says. "That's why the policy is important. And the best time to establish a policy is when you don't need to call an executive session."

It is also crucial, if the CEO is not present, that the CEO be provided with a summary of the session immediately after the meeting—and that the session is held with his or her support. "If the CEO agrees he or she shouldn't be there, that's good," Walker says. "Most important is a strong trust relationship between the CEO and the board. As long as that trust exists, the CEO [remains] an important player by not appearing to be in conflict."

Let 'Em Talk

That's certainly the way Jeffrey Selberg, president and CEO of Denver's Exempla Healthcare, has played it.

"The assumption that unless there is a problem [with the CEO] the board has nothing to talk about [privately] is a misconception about executive sessions," Selberg says. "You'd like to think that the board could talk about anything with the CEO in the room. It should work that way, but I've realized over the past two years that, in order for the board to develop itself as a coherent team, there has to be time when the board [members] talk to just each other. I have no fear about that. CEOs get nervous when executive session is doing the work that the CEO should do."

Selberg believes that trustees "talk more and don't defer to anyone" in executive session and are more likely to ask a wider range of questions. This very much depends on the skills of the board chair, he adds, who must be a good facilitator in establishing the goals of the session's discussion.

"So many times [during a board meeting] management comes in, makes presentations, motions are passed—there's very little time in that process for board members to share their ideas or to ask if strategies and staff/administration relationships are aligned with mission, vision and values. If it's done in a trustworthy manner, it can be useful—[as long as] it's not a complaint session."

Ultimately, there is not much point in trying to fight the use of executive sessions, he adds. "If the CEO figures out a way to not have executive session, what do you think is happening in the parking lot [after the meeting]?" Selberg asks. "Kitchen counter and parking lot conversations take all the wind out of a board. [Those conversations] will happen one way or another, so you might as well have an organized system. If trustees say 'The usual methods are not working, I'm going to do a workaround,' that's a nightmare for a CEO."

COG member Virgil McDonald, chair of Fort Washington (Maryland) Medical Center, knows exactly what Selberg is talking about. In his earlier years as a trustee, the "executive session" was always held in the parking lot after the meeting. McDonald says it was a reaction to an overbearing management style coupled with the need for a stronger chair who could make sure trustees got their chance to speak. As a result, McDonald is more firm than ever that the board "must be able to ask tough questions, get answers and make decisions for the betterment of the community. . . . We needed to change as we did. . . . We made it abundantly clear [with his current CEO] that we would have a strong and involved board, and we would talk things through on our own [in periodic executive sessions] and let him know [what we discussed]."

Beyond avoiding such drama, however, McDonald thinks executive session is an important tool to help boards "coalesce" and grow into their roles. "When I came onto the board, there was a lot I didn't know," McDonald explains. "I was retired, and the language from my job was [used] differently [in the hospital board context]. I missed a lot of what was going on because I didn't understand the language." McDonald thinks executive session can be "reassuring," particularly for new trustees, as a forum for speaking openly and asking basic questions, with the chair bearing the responsibility for keeping everyone equally involved and moving forward in a clear direction.

Executive sessions can benefit the timid as well as the newcomer, Selberg believes. "There are quiet CEOs and dynamic CEOs, and sometimes the conversation is best when the strongest advocate [for a topic] is not there," Selberg says. "I feel like I have a lot of credibility with my board, but there are times [when] that's a liability if they accept my ideas without discussion."

He does not think executive session should be a part of every board agenda but, rather, a mutually agreed-upon decision by the CEO and the chair as the upcoming agenda is determined—whenever "it's time to take the temperature of the board" for clarity and team-building on key strategies.

This kind of discussion can make for a stronger, smarter board, Haeder believes.

"The more the board has its own view, the more savvy it will be, and management will see that," he says. "Executive session is based on free thought. There's no worry about stepping on the CEO's toes . . . and [governance] is not about individual feelings. What you have to do [as a trustee] is deliver excellent health care to your community, and you can do it better with the support of executive sessions to talk freely."

Selberg adds: "The key purpose of an executive session is to draw individuals out and develop team-building through give-and-take conversation. It's inquiry as much as advocacy. The board puts together a much fuller understanding of what [its] own concerns are. Once you have expressed your concerns and had them addressed, then you can fully support [management] decisions."

He concludes, "These conversations are rare, they're great to have and the board needs to have more of them. The issues are so complex now—the board must fully vet them, get different perspectives. Highly effective boards are more thorough and more committed as a result. If that takes executive sessions, how could anyone say it's a bad outcome?"

Tough Love: Ten Questions to Ask Your CEO

By Paul B. Hofmann
and Wanda J. Jones

If your board is typical, there is an unspoken agreement between management and trustees to let management bring issues to the board for discussion. This gives CEOs control over timing and process while not requiring the board to expend a lot of energy searching out problems. In exchange, the board will pay attention to the issues of the day and generally support management's recommendations. After all, the CEO has a major role in trustee selection and orientation to achieve just this level of predictability and comfort.

The tacit understanding among trustees is that CEOs may not be telling the board all that they know or worry about, especially if they do not yet know what to do or if they believe it will unduly worry the board. In this atmosphere, the highest risk is not what is on the table but those subjects that are out of sight, unaddressed.

The following ten questions are a starting point for a new relationship between the board and management—one where the trustees

---

Paul B. Hofmann, Dr.P.H., is senior vice president of Aon Consulting's health care industry practice and chairman of New Century Healthcare Institute, San Francisco. Wanda J. Jones, M.P.H., is president of New Century Healthcare Institute.

can probe for areas of risk in keeping with their fiduciary responsibility to the public. The list follows a hierarchy of importance.

Level I: Manage against Increasing Risk and Declining Revenues

Question 1. What are the main areas of risk in the future, especially in regard to the different rates of change in revenues and costs, and what are our compensating strategies for each?

Corollaries. On which external organizations are we most dependent (e.g., health plans, government payers, individual physicians or medical groups)? On what are our relationships based? How secure are they? What is our contingency plan in the event that any relationship fails? Are we equally adept at managing both revenues and costs?

Question 2. How and when will we adjust expenses to revenues (at the same time, after the fact or in anticipation? by cuts, redesign or reprogramming?)?

Corollaries. How do we protect our quality standards? How do we promote those standards to payers? How do we demonstrate that high quality is cost effective? How do we separate the issue of quality performance from the accusation that price negotiation is all about professional and staff income and corporate profits? Do we give consistent messages to our staff or do we require them to keep quality high while starving them for resources? What do they think? Are we preserving uneconomical programs because of resistance from physicians, staff, unions or the community? How can we position ourselves to make sound resource decisions in a timely, open way?

Question 3. What is the status of our reserve accounts, and how are we protecting them? What is our policy for use of these reserves?

Corollaries. Are we using money earned from patient care activities to invest in nonpatient care activities, such as purchase of medical practices or creation of health plans? If so, how can these investments be returned to our reserves? Do we have a policy concerning the level of reserves we should maintain relative to our risk exposure?

Level II: Capture and Hold Market Share

Question 4. Are we gaining or losing market share—that is, do major payers consider us an essential provider? Why? What is our strategy for attaining a stronger buyer-seller negotiating position?

Corollaries. Do employers and consumers know which delivery system is included in their plans? Do they know enough about us to insist that we be included? What is our reputation with health plans? Why? How can we enhance it? How do we measure market share (share of hospital admissions, share of health plan contracts/enrollees and/or share of the regional health care dollar)?

Are we paying attention to the market share of consumer-paid health care (e.g., for complementary care therapies and plastic surgery, not just insured health care)? Do we still consider only the medical staff our market, or do we now understand how to treat health plans and buyers as our market, along with the general public?

Level III: Restructure and Redesign

Question 5. What proportion of management's work is spent on maintaining the status quo compared with building the next-generation delivery system? Does management have a 5- to 10-year vision of how health care services should be redesigned? Are projects based on delivery redesign, or are they rehousing old concepts?

Corollaries. Does management accept that one role of this organization is to be a community partner in the redesign of health care delivery? Has it added to its own skill mix? Has it engaged with community organizations? Has it brought out the leadership potential in its professional staffs and on this board? Does it demonstrate an understanding of the early trends that hint at how the health care system is being restructured from the outside?

Question 6. In the same time period that costs are being cut, is innovation being protected and preserved?

Corollaries. Is management encouraging innovation in both operations and clinical programs? Is innovation being driven by population need or provider competition or only by technology? What are the barriers to innovation and what is being done to reduce or remove those barriers? Is there congruence between operations and finance on the need to protect innovation? Is the organization geared to learning and changing rapidly, or is innovation slow, tentative and painful? How can the board show its interest in continued innovation as a broad business strategy?

Level IV: Manage Key Relationships

Question 7. What are the organization's key relationships—those that can either support or hinder our development or longevity? What is the status of those relationships? How do we manage them (consider both internal and external relationships, local and nonlocal)?

Corollaries. Are we geared for cooperation with our primary external partners, or is there an atmosphere of self-protection, competition or fear of government's role? Do our internal stakeholders understand the nature of our external relationships, especially buyers and payers? Is there a shared understanding of general health care economics as a basis for mutual planning and cooperation? Do we have plans for improving our perceived value to organizations that we consider valuable to us? Are there relationships that are too costly to sustain in their present form?

Question 8. What are the ethical foundations of our relationships and behaviors? How do we know how well we are maintaining our standards? Are there areas where we are at ethical risk? Are we open with the public about issues the public considers important to it?

Corollaries. Do we scan for the ethical breaches of others as a signal to audit our own practices? Do we have a "crisis management" policy that favors prompt disclosure and problem solving (e.g., billing abuses, mistreatment of patients or an infectious outbreak)? How recently has an ethics audit been conducted?

Level V: Advocate for the Community

Question 9. Do we see ourselves as advocates for the health of the community? If so, how do we fulfill this role? Does the community expect us to represent its interests? To whom?

Corollaries. Are we skilled in interpreting our own experience in community health terms (prevalence of diseases of poverty, for example, or diseases produced from addictions or the environment or diseases related to stress and depression)? Do we view advocacy as the responsibility of other organizations and not our own? Do we expect management will make time for this role? Do we assume the medical staff will advocate as it sees broad health care problems? Are there areas that affect the public in which we may be practicing benign neglect? How do we show the public that we care as much about meeting its needs as we do about our own survival or financial success?

Question 10. Do we contribute to public policy development in health care as we see the increase in public distrust and the growth of activism toward more regulation? If so, how and in what areas?

Corollaries. If we were standing outside looking in at our work, knowing what we know about how health care works, what changes in public policy would be in the public interest? Do we take on the responsibility of educating our publics so policy decisions are at least better informed? Are we open about sharing data and helping with their interpretation? Do we know how to make allies of the media and elected officials? Is the board useful to the organization in translating health care policy proposals to its home organizations and public bodies?

If, over the course of a year, the board's agenda could address these questions in some reasonable order and then visit them again, its positive influence on the course of the organization would greatly increase. All of these questions would signal to management that the board is ready to see the organization through some rough waters—that management need not be reticent to bring up worrisome, but crucial, topics.

Executive Sessions as Standard Operating Procedure

By Eric D. Lister, M.D.,
and Carolyn Jacoby Gabbay

Too many violations of the public trust have led to pressure on governing boards everywhere—pressure to oversee management more rigorously, guide more assertively and operate with greater transparency. Many states are moving to require that not-for-profit boards comply with guidelines similar to those in the Sarbanes-Oxley Act for public boards.

Sarbanes-Oxley requires that public directors address the appropriate relationship between the board and the CEO. Decades ago, health care boards were often passive about overseeing their CEOs, who were given almost total authority over managing hospital operations. Accountability structures and evaluation strategies were more casual. At their worst, such boards were seen as "mushrooms"—kept in the dark by domineering CEOs who were not eager to be accountable to their boards. Of course, many of those boards were complicit in that arrangement.

Eric Lister, M.D., is managing director of Ki Associates and a principal in Healthsure Consultants, Temple, Texas. Carolyn Jacoby Gabbay, J.D., is a partner in the Boston office of the law firm of Nixon Peabody LLP.

Steadily, through the application of regulatory pressure, the guidance of governance experts and the advice of governance literature, this dynamic has changed. Uninvolved boards are now a rarity. Clearer guidelines around the CEO evaluation and board self-evaluation process have resulted in a board-CEO relationship typified by openness and explicit accountabilities.

Independent Trustees and the Balance of Power

Two powerful forces tend to tilt the ideal balance of power between the board and the CEO in a health care organization. The first of these forces has to do with the complexity of health care. Arcane reimbursement mechanisms, reams of regulatory guidelines, abstruse scientific principles and a system designed around autonomous providers all make the health care industry unique. Lay trustees tell us that they are often perplexed by these issues and struggle with how to exercise the appropriate level of fiduciary responsibility.

The second force relates to the volunteer status of health care boards. Compensation for health care trustees is rare, and the time demands—for studying board informational packets, obtaining the necessary education, participating in committee meetings, fulfilling ambassadorial duties—often tax even the most well-intentioned and responsible trustees.

For these reasons, the powers and autonomy of the CEO are constantly at risk of expanding excessively, while the authority of the board is at risk of contracting inappropriately—all without the conscious intent of either party.

This imbalance makes it difficult for many boards to raise and discuss concerns or develop goals for the CEO, because the trustees are often simply too dependent on their CEOs for direction. And when boards' concerns remain buried, one of three things can happen:

- Concerns melt away as new information reassures trustees.
- Concerns fester, giving rise to subliminal currents of unease, becoming the stuff of "parking lot conversations" and vague, but pervasive, tensions and doubts.
- Concerns escalate and surface as a push to remove the CEO, who is often shocked since he/she never learned the extent of board dissatisfaction.

When, in response to rising tensions, the board moves to meet in executive session (i.e., without the CEO or any other internal members) in a way that seems to be out of the blue, tensions can skyrocket. The stakes are so high—both for the organization and personally for the CEO—and the atmosphere so charged that, unless the board has decided to make a change in leadership, great efforts must be made to reassure the CEO. And, if there are grave concerns about leadership, rarely do CEOs tell us that they are given enough time and information to address board concerns before it is too late.

Benefits of Regular Executive Sessions

To avoid these problems, we urge a greater level of ongoing candor and spontaneity between boards and their CEOs to ensure that subtle concerns surface promptly, with the right mixture of candor and grace. Such an environment would allow dialogue, assist the CEO in his or her personal development and lead to early problem resolution. However, the factors described above can make it difficult for boards to implement this good, if somewhat naive, counsel.

In addition to urging candor, we think that it is wise to create a structure that makes it easier to follow our advice. Establishing a protocol for regularly scheduled executive sessions can be very useful in helping boards and CEOs achieve the right level of candor, while removing the stigma and fear associated with "surprise" executive sessions.

Most boards already schedule an annual executive session to discuss the CEO's performance evaluation and compensation. We suggest conducting such sessions quarterly. Some CEOs blanche at this recommendation. They tell us that the board can always go into executive session if it wishes, but that regular sessions without the CEO would be a sign of distrust and would set the stage for "end runs" around the chief executive. Our experience, however, has been quite the opposite.

Harvey Yorke is an enthusiastic supporter of the practice. "This process gets 'stuff' out on the table," Yorke says. "When there is no opportunity for that to happen, I think a CEO is at greater risk of an issue that is minor growing into one that is major . . . simply because there is no forum to get it out." For more than a decade,

Yorke has served as president and CEO of Southwestern Vermont Health Care, a Bennington-based system comprising one acute care hospital, satellite offices and a long-term care facility. During the last several years, the system board has conducted monthly executive sessions.

By moving "parking lot conversations" into the boardroom and giving trustees a proper forum in which to raise any nagging concerns they may have—not just about the CEO but about anything—the board fulfills its fiduciary duty more responsibly and creates a platform from which to confront issues at an early stage, when they are likely to be more easily managed.

"The meetings are simply an opportunity to determine *if* there are any issues relative to performance; not a signal that there *are* any [issues]," says Yorke.

For regularly scheduled executive sessions to be effective, the board chair shoulders substantial responsibility for making the process constructive and effective. The chair will need to:

- Be clear about the agenda and sensitive to any implicit concerns.
- Insist that all present use the session to air any and all current concerns, while making it equally clear that the sessions are not occasions to rehash old or chronic grudges, idle speculation or casual gossip.
- Foster sufficiently full discussion of any issues that do surface so they can either be eliminated or lead to a specific plan for further action.
- Following the session, debrief immediately with the CEO and frame any items that need research, further discussion, or formal follow-up.
- Keep sessions short and focused.

When the procedure for raising issues and dealing with them is solidly in place, the board chair is in a vastly improved position to coach and counsel the CEO.

According to Yorke, "Coaching is a key responsibility of the board chair, but there can be no coaching if it is not okay to candidly discuss CEO performance, or if it only gets discussed once a year during formal performance assessment processes. . . . This philosophy at the top of the organization plays a significant . . . role in building a culture committed to candid feedback and performance improvement."

The benefits of regular executive sessions, when they are conducted in the spirit of a genuine desire to improve board-CEO relations, are well worth the inevitable discomfort that comes with embracing a new and different practice.

PART THREE

CEO Leadership

Orchestrating the New Leadership: What It Takes to Be a CEO Today

By Patrick Plemmons

In a few terrible moments on the morning of September 11, our world changed forever, and one of the more striking changes came in how we viewed our leaders. Suddenly, our nation's priorities and needs changed dramatically, and we found we wanted and valued a whole different type of leader, with different skills and personal characteristics. Fortunately, President Bush, Mayor Giuliani of New York City and many other lesser-known leaders rose to the occasion and showed us character traits we had not seen previously.

The lesson is clear—when the basic rules of the game change significantly, we require a different type of leadership. Admittedly, changes in the hospital industry have not been as sudden as those the nation experienced last September, but the field has experienced sweeping and almost continuous change over the past 10 to 15 years. And the hospital CEO's job has had to change accordingly. When a board has to recruit a new CEO, what skills and qualities should it seek? And given the tremendous complexity and difficulty

---

Patrick Plemmons is a vice-president in the Atlanta office of executive search firm Tyler & Co.

of leading a hospital today, how long can any CEO hope to be effective? Does an effective leader have a "life span" in one organization, after which he or she needs to move on?

The Good Old Days

David Hannan, the CEO of South Shore Hospital in South Weymouth, Massachusetts, remembers an easier era of hospital leadership before the mid-1980s when DRGs were first implemented: "It was easy to run a hospital. It was a cost-plus environment, and you could function in isolation and get by. You just had to be a cheerleader and adequate supply sergeant. Now things are more global and interconnected, and you must be a leader in the real sense of the word," he says.

The complexity of leading health care organizations has been increasing incrementally since DRGs, managed care and, most recently, the Balanced Budget Amendment. Employees, especially nurses, have unionized, and physicians have become disaffected and contentious as their own profession has come under increasing scrutiny and attack.

Certainly, definitions of *leadership* are subject to interpretation. Faced with declining margins, workforce shortages and seemingly relentless pressures from patients and payers alike, the "kinder and gentler" leader has had to toughen up.

Joe Swedish, CEO of Denver-based Centura Health System, agrees that the business of providing health care has changed and not necessarily for the better. "This business does not have the gentility it used to have," says Swedish. "And the customer today is markedly different from earlier days in hospitals."

He adds that with the current emphasis on access to capital and financial issues, a CEO must have much stronger financial skills now than in the past. "I see the job today as a combination of leadership and technical skills. Finance has been a critical part of my job at Centura. I am passionate about performance metrics, and to implement those, you must understand the technical aspects of running the organization. I can't afford to be disconnected from operations and function exclusively at a strategic level," Swedish says. Since he was brought into Centura to carry out "a pure [i.e., financial] turnaround," such a strong emphasis on financial skills has been an important part of his job description. And it brings up another important point: job descriptions are not monolithic, but differ according to the needs of the organization at any given time.

"Different phases of organizational life require a different CEO job description," says Swedish. "Be realistic as a board about where your organization is on the continuum and what kind of leadership you need." For many board members, this is a challenging exercise because they are relatively new to the organization and may not have a historical perspective. Still, boards must take the time to learn where the organization is today if they hope to identify a CEO who can lead them effectively tomorrow.

The Vision Thing

For South Shore's Hannan, the key element of real leadership is vision. "You must have a vision for the organization, and then you implement that vision by getting good people [to work with you], teaching them, listening to them and learning from them." Jim Hinton, CEO of Presbyterian Healthcare Services, based in Albuquerque, New Mexico, also believes in the importance of a CEO's vision: "The job is to create a rational plan [i.e., vision] for the future of the organization and make sure that the operational chassis and indicators are in sync with that plan." Gary Strack, the former CEO and principal architect of the Orlando (Florida) Regional Healthcare System, agrees. "A CEO must see further and have greater cognitive ability and greater emotional maturity than those he is leading," he says.

But vision alone is insufficient for good CEO leadership. To complement a clear and far-reaching vision, the CEO also needs an intimate understanding of how to provide and finance health care. Hinton puts it this way: "Your business has to be coherent and focused; most businesses fall down because of a lack of clarity. The focus must be on the organization, not the leader."

Michael Rindler, a former hospital CEO and president of The Rindler Group, a health care leadership and financial performance improvement consulting firm based in Hilton Head Island, South Carolina, agrees. He takes a decidedly dim view of what might be called the "captain-of-industry" model of the hospital CEO, prevalent since the 1970s. In this dated model, the hospital CEO is expected to be running a diversified, vertically integrated business, in which providing health care services is de-emphasized. In actuality, the CEO is preoccupied with system building, acquisition of non–health care businesses, creative financing and corporate staffing. Rindler believes that the CEO of 2002 must "get back to basics and focus on running a better hospital." That means concentrating on high-quality medical care and improved medical staff leadership and achieving at least a 3 percent operating margin.

Being There

Leading, inspiring and motivating the organization's employees were vital to all of the CEOs with whom we spoke, but Sue Brody, CEO of Bayfront Medical Center, St. Petersburg, Florida, takes it a step further. Brody, the recent ACHE Young Healthcare Executive of the Year, says, "You have to personify the institution; you have to be its physical presence. You should be visible and accessible to all the groups and people in the organization so they know they can come to you for advice or reassurance, or just to be heard." Of course, in a stand-alone hospital, such as Bayfront, this accessibility is still possible. In a system, especially a large, multistate one, it's impossible for a CEO to be physically available to all staff. So the system CEO must rely on a management team and processes to unify the organization.

In order to benefit most from other people's talents, Presbyterian Healthcare's Hinton still believes in constant communication from the leader. "Far and away, the most important skill of the CEO is understanding the importance of, and carrying out, active communication," he says. Sue Brody agrees: "A large part of my job is inspirational and motivational. How you communicate to people, in all settings, is so important, maybe the most important thing." Gary Strack adds, "Seventy percent of the [CEO's] job is creating a climate that generates mutual trust and respect so people can learn, grow and develop. You have to force a planning process and set goals and objectives. Give people a challenge so they can stretch, and give them support by training and leading. Challenge is toxic without support. Create an inclusive organization—open and non-secretive. Use the minds and energy of your people and drive fear out of the system."

Encouraging CEO Leadership Qualities

To help develop CEO and senior management leadership skills and qualities, you can do the following:

- Ensure that job descriptions explicitly detail desired leadership qualities and behaviors. These should be emphasized at least as much as technical skills and experience.
- Use leadership criteria in CEO formal and informal evaluations. By including leadership effectiveness in the formal evaluation process, you signal the importance of these skills to the organization's overall success. To be most effective, leadership skill evaluation should be continuous, not just a part of the formal review.
- To really gain the CEO's full attention, link leadership goal achievement to financial rewards. Bonuses can be a powerful motivator for leaders to further develop their skills.
- Include leadership qualities in the organization's mission and values statements and in the formal strategic planning process. Because so much of leadership depends on developing the optimal organizational culture, this action will emphasize the importance of leadership to both internal and external stakeholders in the organization.
- Give leadership substantial weight in the hiring decision whenever the organization recruits a new CEO or other senior manager. This will not only add to an overall culture of leadership, but will also reinforce to existing managers the importance of leadership values.
- Include leadership topics in the board's continuing education. Trustees and the CEO can attend seminars or conferences about leadership, and experts in leadership may also be invited to speak to the board.
- Model the behavior you seek to encourage in your CEO. By the questions you ask, by the issues you hold most important, by all the contributions to governance you make, you can be a positive role model in stimulating the CEO to be the best possible leader he or she can be.

Brody also notes the importance of the CEO's energy and enthusiasm. "Energy is so important—or maybe it's just stamina. You have to keep going and stay positive and consistent. That's what people respond to best." But in uncertain times, consistency often falls victim to crisis management. The predictable leader becomes unpredictable. Unfortunately, those are precisely the times when it's most important for CEOs to be consistent about what they say and do.

But CEOs do not have to have all the answers. In fact, Hannan notes, humility is a helpful quality. "It's much more important to know how to ask really good questions and then know if the answers make sense," adds Brody. Ray Budrys, CEO of Craven Regional Medical Center, New Bern, North Carolina, uses this metaphor: "The CEO is an orchestra conductor. You need to know what a violin looks like and how it should sound, but you don't need to be a violin virtuoso."

Gary Strack sums it up nicely: "The higher up you go, who you are matters a lot more than what you know."

That's why teamwork is important to all the CEOs with whom we talked. Hospitals are extremely complex organizations, and the demands placed on them are so great that no one person can hope to solve every problem. The CEO cannot be seen as someone who has all the answers. Indeed, one of the most important functions of a CEO is choosing a team of outstanding senior managers and supporting and developing them. As Jim Hinton says, "If you are a set of solutions looking for problems to solve, you are going to be ineffective in short order. The success of our organization is directly related to the activities of our senior team, and all of them are involved at the board level."

Sue Brody believes that people respond as much with their hearts as with their minds. "The people in this organization are mission-driven, but I don't think that's why they do things. They do things for other people in the institution."

View from the Boardroom

Larry Davis, M.D., board chairman at Bayfront Medical Center, believes that 70 percent of a hospital CEO's job description revolves around personality. He sees the CEO's role today as providing a vision for where the medical center is heading and putting together a strong, autonomous management team. Interpersonal relations with physicians are also a very important part of the job. Basically, he says, "a CEO makes decisions, works with people and gets things done."

Lottie Kurcz is a senior vice president with FirstHealth, a managed care company in Chicago, and chair of Holy Cross Hospital in Chicago. After a difficult search process, Holy Cross hired a new CEO about six months ago. The hospital needed a CEO who could develop and implement a strategic plan—someone who could act quickly and decisively on tough issues. The board struggled with how to evaluate and measure the candidates' real operating style. It's much easier to get a handle on financial measures or number of employees or similar "hard" metrics. But Kurcz believes the board hired the right CEO because it did not rely primarily on interviews, but conducted broad, in-depth referencing.

The importance of references cannot be overemphasized. In our experience, it is virtually the only way to thoroughly evaluate and predict leadership skills and styles. And it is vital that whoever checks references understands the context in which the candidate has operated. A skilled interviewer, with in-depth industry knowledge and contacts, can develop the best picture of a prospective CEO's personality, behaviors and track record with people.

It's easy for a charismatic candidate who is a skillful communicator to fool interviewers. In fact, there have been several recent high-profile instances of résumé fraud by senior executives in the corporate world.

Careful reference checking is one of the best ways to uncover dishonesty among job seekers. And the best way to conduct these checks is by using the "360-degree" method, which entails talking to superiors, subordinates and peers. Most important, it means not relying on a list of references furnished by the candidate. The board needs to develop its own list of key references based on the candidate's experience and current situation. If a reference is "off limits," there needs to be a very good reason. The board needs to look for themes across references, and when a problem surfaces in one reference, it should be tested against others. A search committee should not settle for generalities—it needs to press for specifics and be prepared with questions that are germane to the specific recruitment.

Where Are the CEOs?

There was no shortage of qualified candidates in Holy Cross's search. "I would be very surprised if there were not a lot of qualified people just waiting for a chance to run [your] hospital," says Bayfront's Davis. "They are out there; just give the young ones a chance."

Jim Hinton was 36 when he became CEO of a multihospital system, and he sees no shortage of leaders. "I see lots of capable young leaders out there," he says. "Granted, we're not seeing the same

---

Evaluating CEO Leadership

As a board or CEO evaluation committee, first decide on the specific criteria you want to evaluate, and then develop questions that will give you the information you need to reach an informed opinion. This need not be an overly formal and structured exercise. Just come up with a few questions that deal with the most important aspects of leadership. For example: Do employees feel valued? What is the organization's reputation in the community and in the health care field? Has the CEO assembled and developed a strong management team? How visible and accessible is the CEO? Questions such as these, when posed to the right people, will develop a true picture of the CEO's leadership effectiveness. So who are the right people to ask?

For starters, ask those who know best—employees. And not just senior managers, but employees at every level. If the CEO is doing an outstanding job of creating a positive culture where employees feel empowered and valued and where everyone is working toward shared goals, staff will confirm it. Don't delegate this task to someone in human resources or just send out a survey. Trustees should talk directly with a cross-section of employees to get a true picture of the CEO's leadership effectiveness.

People outside the organization can be helpful as well. Former employees will sometimes be more honest than current staff, and vendors, consultants and other external parties can offer valuable insights too.

Continued →

career paths as before." Today, CEOs are coming from the ranks of planners, nursing, human resources and even from boards of trustees (see the article "Your CEO: Are You Short-Staffed or Shortsighted?" starting on page 71 of this book). Operations is no longer the sole training ground for hospital leaders. David Hannan advises, "Don't be afraid to look in nontraditional places; one-third of my senior team [was originally] from outside of health care. Leadership skills are not much different in this field from any other." Trustees are advised to be open-minded to both youth and change, experts agree.

Any evaluation of CEO leadership must also include the medical staff. Of all the relationships a health care CEO must cultivate, his or her relationship with the medical staff is the most important to the organization's success. Physicians are usually very frank when expressing their opinions about the CEO, and their insights can be most useful in assessing top leadership.

Industry rankings and awards can also aid leadership evaluation. For instance, *Working Mother* magazine presents an annual award to the top 100 corporations that are especially supportive of issues important to their female employees. Bayfront Medical Center in St. Petersburg, Florida, won this award in 2000 and in previous years, indicating that Bayfront's CEO places a high priority on creating a welcoming, supportive employee environment. Such actions are one of the hallmarks of effective CEO leadership.

Evaluating CEO leadership is a task that trustees should not delegate, but there are times when outside expertise can be helpful. Executive search consultants, management psychologists or management consultants can bring an outsider's perspective and many years of experience to the evaluation process.

But in the end, trustees themselves must make the final judgments when evaluating CEO leadership.

"I think you are seeing a generation passing, and they might think that they can't be replaced. Maybe it's a case of boards not giving young people a chance," says Bayfront's Brody. During the many tough years hospitals have endured, it could be expected that boards would be more risk-averse in choosing leaders and would opt for the most-experienced leaders. But Brody also points out that "it's more acceptable now to 'have a life' and to balance work and family. I'm not sure the existing [CEO] leadership buys into that yet."

The Time of Your Life

How long can a CEO be effective in the same organization? Brody thinks "there are waves of organizational life, and you have to recognize the new ones coming along and reenergize people and yourself along new lines." Michael Rindler is more specific: "Ten years is the optimum tenure. That takes you through two complete strategic planning cycles. After five years, you start facing the consequences of decisions you have made." Craven Regional's Budrys is equally precise. "Five to seven years is probably the optimum life span of a CEO in one organization. Medical staff conflicts will inevitably grow over this time and reach critical mass. If you're trying to do the right things for the organization and community, you will eventually face serious conflicts." Gary Strack sees CEO tenure as a structural issue. "The problems in leading a hospital organization are so systemic that doing the right thing for the institution, over time, [leads to] falling on your sword," he says. Hannan sees the CEO's organizational life span as being divided into five-year segments. He believes that the first five years are spent serving the community and hospital; the second five trying to realign the medical staff; and "during the next five years, you need to reinvent yourself or get out."

Even though the exact timetable may be debatable, it's clear that there is some effective life span in which a CEO can optimize leadership and performance. Just as organizations go through life cycles or waves, so too, it appears, do CEOs. There is no "one-size-fits-all" model of hospital leadership and no date carved in stone for when it makes sense to move on.

FirstHealth's Lottie Kurcz believes that the two most important responsibilities a board has are choosing a CEO and then ensuring that he or she remains the right leader as the organization changes. David Hannan agrees: "Leadership is a long-term thing, and it takes courage." Boards can show their own courage by seeking out CEOs who are true leaders and by giving young leaders a chance to take their place on the stage.

And what characterizes a true leader? The message from the CEOs represented here is clear—the "softer" skills are the ones that ensure effective leadership. Vision, focus, integrity, communication, consistency, energy, team building—these are some of the essential skills of today's CEO. The challenge for boards is to recognize and measure such inexact skills as best they can when evaluating existing and prospective CEOs. It's not easy, but it can and must be done.

Your CEO: Are You Short-Staffed or Shortsighted?

By Laurie Larson

Are you ready for yet another health care crisis? Truth or rumor—we're running out of hospital CEOs. You decide. "We are observing an impending leadership shortage at the CEO level," says Christopher Press, partner with Morgan Healthcare Consulting in Atlanta. "The argument is that there's not enough talent to promote and that people are burned out and leaving health care, but I'm a little bit of a contrarian—why is there a shortage?"

Larry Tyler, president of Tyler & Company, an Atlanta-based health care executive search firm, doesn't see a crisis, but he does see the CEO's job changing dramatically.

"This used to be an easy business, but now it's extremely complicated. There's a bigger pool—a larger percentage of people applying [to be CEO]—but the percentage of people who can do the job is smaller." That, in and of itself, constitutes a crisis to some experts.

"Yes, there's a crisis—it's [happening] now, and it will get worse," counters Carson Dye, partner with executive search firm Witt Kieffer in Toledo, Ohio. "Ten years ago we could present a list of eight to ten

---

Laurie Larson is *Trustee*'s associate editor.

candidates [to a client] versus two or three today. It's [now] taking us a month longer to fill CEO positions." The reason, he believes, is a profound change over the past decade in a field that maintained the status quo for 25 years, until the "empire building" of the 1990s. Mergers and acquisitions, reimbursement riddles and managed care have reduced the raw numbers of qualified candidates, Dye says, as executives have either left the field from stress or burnout or lacked the complex expertise needed for the new system. Others think that same stress has left the best men and women still standing.

"In my opinion, there is no leadership crisis for the most part," says Arnie Kuypers, president of The Kuypers Company, a health care executive search firm in Plano, Texas. Not as many CEOs are leaving the field now as they did three or four years ago.

"I think most CEOs have adjusted—those who wanted out were culled out," Kuypers says. "The bench strength is out there, but you have to know what you are looking for." Health system CEOs are actually managing revenue dollars more intelligently than CEOs in other industries, he believes. But it remains a question of quality, not quantity.

"It's the ability to find the right people who are capable," Kuypers says. CEOs today need broader skill sets, including an in-depth knowledge of compliance, managed care, strategy, quality mandates and strategies of system and relationship building.

Broaden Your Search

Press thinks such a broad palette of skills should open the field to a wider and less traditional range of candidates.

"Leadership is [being] too narrowly defined," he says. "In many industries, a person will rotate through several key positions in the organization, having learned the business from all sides. Health care doesn't do that." A typical path for a CEO begins as a department head, followed by becoming a vice president of operations, then chief operating officer, and then CEO, he observes.

"A CEO's job is not operations; it's strategy, policy, relationships and finance," Press says. "When a business is as complex as health care, wouldn't you want everyone to know each other's area of business?" Through their performance appraisals, boards should motivate CEOs to encourage a wide range of applicants for all jobs within the hospital, he thinks. "People are a competitive asset," Press says. "You always want [employees] to know where their work comes from and where it goes, the impact of their work on others."

At Witt Kieffer, Dye sees more CEOs coming out of finance and patient care—there are currently 135 physician CEOs in the United States, he estimates, with more to come. "We will see more physicians ascend to these positions—lots of doctors are getting MBAs and MHAs [master's in health administration]—it's one of the fastest growing graduate program areas in the country."

The American College of Healthcare Executives, Chicago, has seen an "enormous growth" in physician members, and Dye thinks it's a good trend because physicians "know how to get things done at 3 A.M."

Financial and clinical experts make good candidates, Press agrees, but someone with a marketing or human resources background, for example, could also lead through innovation or by understanding employees.

The Making of a Health System CEO

Ron Hogan is one such success story. A trustee at St. Joseph's Health System in Atlanta since 1990, he became board chair in 1992 and CEO in 1995. He came to St. Joseph's after serving 27 years with Georgia-Pacific Corp., the last three as president and chief operating officer. His transition from one of the world's leading manufacturers of paper and building products to health care was unexpected, but logical.

Health care costs were skyrocketing at Georgia-Pacific, and Hogan wanted to know why, so he sought an opportunity to become a health care trustee. He became chair as St. Joseph's was preparing for a potential merger. Suspecting their jobs might be sacrificed, the CEO and the chief operating and financial officer all found new positions. But the merger didn't happen, and Hogan was asked to step in as interim CEO while the board sought a replacement.

Catholic Health East, which owns St. Joseph's, then took a good look at its "temporary" leader (recently in charge of 60,000 employees at Georgia-Pacific and with five years of board experience) and asked Hogan to stay. His broad management background and a hands-on knowledge of volatility won him the job, he thinks.

"I have dealt with change throughout my career. The forest products industry has gone from a competitive to a regulatory industry, with government involvement in environmental issues versus reimbursement issues [and regulations] in health care," Hogan says.

The Search

Regardless of where candidates come from, however, the responsibility for finding the right one rests where it always has: with the board.

As a starting point, Dye thinks it's important that everyone who will be directly affected by the new CEO be consulted before the search begins. "Get consensus among board members up front," Dye says. "Make sure everyone agrees what the CEO should be."

Next, he thinks the defining question that boards should ask any candidate is, "Have you done this before?" and that question should be honed to immediate needs.

"Boards should ask themselves, 'Exactly what do we need done?' Within the first 12 to 15 months of a CEO's tenure, specific objectives should be set [and] achieved," Dye says. He gives the example of settling a dispute between surgeons who may leave and open their own ambulatory surgery center if the hospital can't negotiate with them. "Find the candidates who have faced your specific problems and solved them. The second test is chemistry and fit."

What that means to Dye, Kuypers and other executive search experts is that CEOs are, and should be, still coming up through hospital operations.

"I've been asked to find candidates outside health care, but they don't get hired," Kuypers says. "You need that knowledge base. There's a credibility that managing assets gives you."

Count (and Keep) Your Blessings

But the best choice of all, they agree, is not having to find a new CEO in the first place. In other words, if you like the CEO you have, do whatever you can to keep him or her.

Dye predicts that over the next five years, more CEOs will retire than in the past 15. Boards need to ask themselves the blunt question: "How easily could our CEO leave, and what would we have to pay his successor if he [or she] left?"

"You have to pay competitively to really have the advantage," Kuypers says. "If you don't want to lose people, stay on top of compensation surveys and find out how much [executives] are being paid."

"You will always pay more for a new person . . . much more," Dye says. Pay raises and supplemental executive retirement plans (SERPs), which provide more pay at retirement if CEOs commit to a longer contract, make more sense, as does considering an internal candidate, who might be happy with less money than a new person for the opportunity to move up.

Whether or not your CEO tells you his or her future plans, Dye thinks that some simple demographics may be worth considering.

"If you have a CEO who's about 50 years old and has been there for five or six years, he is a prime person to leave," partly because of where he is in his career and partly because he may have children who have left for college, freeing him up to make changes, Dye says. A 40-something CEO of comparable tenure may be scooped up by a competitor as well, he says—the CEO is young and his or her children are ready for high school, another good transition time.

When a CEO wants to talk about retirement plans or giving the CFO or COO more responsibility, that may also be a signal of impending change, and boards need to pay attention, Dye advises.

Trustees should also keep an eye out for CEO burnout, as complex responsibilities and environmental pressures take their toll. "If your CEO is burned out, look at [giving the CEO] a sabbatical of six months to a year to recharge his or her batteries. Continuity of management is a key characteristic of successful organizations," Kuypers says.

To head off burnout at the pass, he recommends finding CEOs at the "right" stage of their career—a "grow-your-own-CEO" philosophy. The right candidate should come in ready to commit to the organization with an incentive to stay through compensation and SERPs.

A Marketing Perspective

A nontraditional leader of his organization for 13 years, Phil Newbold, CEO of Memorial Health System in South Bend, Indiana, has a bachelor's degree in mathematics, an MBA and an MHA. Between the two advanced degrees, he thinks an MBA is the most valuable one today.

"There are so many financial pressures on CEOs now," Newbold says. "You need a broader and deeper background . . . not so 'hospitalcentric' as an MHA. Now we have more retail, partnerships, outsourcing—more intersections with non–health care principles."

Newbold's health care marketing background first led to a strategic planning position at Children's Hospital in Columbus, Ohio, then to the position of vice president of planning and marketing at Baptist Medical Center in Oklahoma City. From there, he became Memorial's CEO.

Newbold describes Memorial as "an organization on the move," noted for its tithing policy (10 percent of the hospital's annual bottom line after taxes is used for community partnerships) and "community plunges." (The October 1997 article "Up Close and Personal" can be accessed from *Trustee* archives at www.trusteemag.com.)

Newbold believes his greatest strengths are his customer orientation and his ability to differentiate Memorial's quality and services from other systems through "basic marketing principles." Customer service often means making sure that staff, particularly physicians, are getting what they need. In fact, he calls physician relationships "the key to getting ahead in health care."

Succession Is Job One

You also get ahead by planning ahead—that is, succession. Newbold thinks CEOs and boards should talk about their professional development goals as part of their annual evaluation. Kuypers believes succession planning "clearly should be written into the annual objectives for the CEO or it won't get done." Tyler agrees. "CEO selection is the most important thing a board does," he believes.

"Boards need to talk about succession once a year or so," Dye says. "They should ask the CEO: 'Are you going to go? Are you happy?' It really [takes] courage to put it on the table."

Potential internal successors should be trained over several years to gain the breadth and depth of experience they will need—and that candidate list should be short. Having too many potential successors doesn't give anyone the "opportunity to rise above," Kuypers says. "Key accountability can't be split up [among too many people]; it must be given to the heir apparent you have chosen." Choosing an internal candidate sends a great loyalty message to the organization as well, he adds.

Tyler recommends that heir apparents be watched with the following questions in mind: Do they accomplish their current job well? Have they accomplished the objectives they've set for themselves? How are they accomplishing them—is staff happy and do physicians have confidence in them? At each career milestone, these three questions should be asked again.

What Tomorrow's Leaders Need

Tyler thinks CEO flexibility and adaptability cannot be overemphasized in today's market. "It's virtually impossible to control anything anymore," he says. For this reason, CEOs need far better communication skills than before. They have to be better listeners and more careful writers because of instantaneous communication (e-mail). And they have to produce.

"There is a hardworking results orientation [in health care] now. You used to be able to take your time, but now you have to get things accomplished and have something to show immediately," Tyler says. "If you don't work on your short-term [financial goals], there will be no long term." And being quick on their feet may come more easily to executives from a less conservative field.

"I think one of the best things I brought to the job as CEO was not having any baggage from old payment systems and how things used to be done," former trustee Hogan says. "I was uninformed enough to ask questions others had been afraid to ask. Sometimes I'd get different answers than [had been given to CEOs] before as to why we do or don't do something." Putting people first has served him well, too. "How you treat and manage people is the most important [CEO] trait—your staff has to have faith in you."

"Until 15 years ago, hospitals were looking for managers. Now we want leaders," Tyler says. "The world is changing so fast; it's not enough to just go through the motions—you've got to be making something happen. We need someone who has a vision—an idea—and can execute it. CEO leaders will be measured by what they accomplish, not by their number of full-time employees." In addition, true leaders have an intangible quality, according to Newbold.

"Most leadership skills can be taught," Newbold says, "but you cannot change your personality. You're [either] a people person or you're not. Leaders of the future need a passion; they have to be energetic about something. They need a zest for innovation and creativity and a [belief that] it's not [too] expensive to take chances. It doesn't cost a thing to treat patients well and to develop trust."

Leading by Listening: How Scripps Health Turned Defeat Around

By Laurie Larson

It was a tense, action-packed drama that only needed a movie producer. A new health system CEO with a "grand plan" but no backing, steps in and starts making big changes with little discussion—not with his hospital administrators, not with his system board—and most fatally, not with his 2,600 affiliated physicians.

Outraged by a sense of lost independence, shrinking financial resources and most of all, what they perceived as the dismissive secrecy of their new leader, those physicians took to the streets, storming the media, diverting patients to other hospitals and ultimately voicing a vote of no-confidence in their CEO. Angry physicians, particularly organized angry physicians, are a force to be reckoned with—as Scripps Health in San Diego found out in 2000. When the smoke cleared, the CEO was gone and so apparently was Scripps' financial future. Yet today, Scripps is back in the game—and back in the black.

How did they fall so far? And more importantly, how did they bounce back? One word: leadership—first done wrong, then done right.

Laurie Larson is *Trustee*'s associate editor.

Part I: Leading Wrong

The president and CEO who came under fire, Stanley Pappelbaum, M.D., had originally been brought into Scripps in 1996 as the system's "chief transformation officer" to write the system's strategic plan.

Comprising five acute care hospitals in the San Diego area and 12 ambulatory and home health clinics, the not-for-profit, community-based Scripps Health system is well-known as a diagnostic center for cardiology and cancer and runs additional specialty treatment centers for diabetes and addiction treatment, as well as an eye institute and a rehabilitation center. The affiliated Scripps Research Institute leads Scripps' renowned medical research initiatives, and the Scripps Foundation for Medicine and Science raises funds to support both the research institute and the system.

When the previous CEO retired, Pappelbaum was asked to step in, and his transformation recommendations took the form of "Project Scripps," a comprehensive restructuring that placed all hospital, clinic and affiliated medical group contracts under Scripps' corporate ownership.

All physicians would be under the Project Scripps umbrella, and the system would own and administer all their managed care contracts and payments, leveraging better deals than physicians had been able to negotiate on their own. The idea was to dominate the local market by working directly with payers.

In addition, Project Scripps planned to develop several "systems of excellence," researching best practices in cardiology, oncology and other specialties and implementing them at all their hospitals. The project had a $250 million "strategic capital fund" to be shared by all the hospitals as the various systems of excellence evolved.

However, Project Scripps was destined to be far from excellent for one glaring reason: it affected all the system's physicians but failed to engage the majority of them. Pappelbaum had handpicked all the physicians who would lead the systems of excellence research, ignoring and thereby alienating the elected hospital medical leadership. That only fueled the larger fear among physicians that they were losing control over their contracts and their autonomy through the Project Scripps payer setup—and that no one was listening.

"Physicians saw the CEO's attempts to organize them as a threat, so they started wreaking havoc," trustee Larry Kline, M.D., explains. However, Pappelbaum did one thing that was very right. He brought in a new chief operating officer named Chris Van Gorder.

"When push came to shove, there was no detailed understanding [by physicians] of Project Scripps," Van Gorder explains. "These medical groups treasured their contracts and they realized that they had lost control of them to the system." Additionally, all the hospitals perceived the strategic planning fund as a bottomless funding source to which they all had equal and unlimited rights. This created yet another "sense of disconnect" as Van Gorder calls it, as each hospital began its research work but could not get funding.

Between the funding stalls, an encroaching loss of medical practice control and rapidly waning confidence in Project Scripps, physicians and hospital staff began to worry that patient care funds were being diverted, that quality was suffering, that equipment was falling apart—and that their CEO didn't want to hear about it. So they turned to the public instead, writing letters to the newspaper, making calls, pointing out unsanitary conditions to the media and telling grateful patients to keep their checkbooks closed.

Ultimately, after a year and a half under Pappelbaum's tenure, five of Scripps' six hospitals (one was closed in 2000), passed a vote of no-confidence in their CEO's leadership, and in May of 2000, he was asked to resign.

Pappelbaum was not entirely surprised. Quoted in the *San Diego Union-Tribune* that May, he said, "One of the toughest jobs in American society is being the CEO of a complex health system. It's tough because the current business models are no longer viable in this changing economic environment." Of his requested resignation, he said, "It's disheartening, but it's what you do if you're an agent of change and if you deeply believe how important change is."

Trustee Frank Panarisi was Scripps' board chair from 2000 to 2002—and saw it all.

"He was a great visionary, but he had no management experience and hadn't worked out the implementation of his plans," Panarisi explains. "He didn't listen to doctors and it didn't come to the board's attention until the no-confidence letter went to the press." About that time, Panarisi got 50 letters from unhappy doctors himself.

"It was a smoldering that finally started burning," Panarisi says. "The board had wanted to support his vision but it took a while to see it wasn't going to work. . . . In hindsight, we should have stepped in a little sooner; we waited too long and let it go too far."

Scripps' board was kept disconnected from the state of affairs as much as staff. Physicians had tried to contact trustees, but the administration would not release their phone numbers. Any questions to leadership were most often answered with a blanket statement that promised well-being and asked everyone for continued support, but gave little detail, Kline says.

Through the credentialing committee, trustees finally heard the first rumblings of dissent, and it was not until they read about it in the papers and found out that donors had been told to withhold contributions that they realized how badly leadership had crumbled.

Van Gorder was asked to serve as interim CEO while the board looked for a replacement. But after a month, he had already effected so much positive change, the board asked him to take the job.

Part II: Leading Right

"I was blessed with support very quickly," Van Gorder says. "I have always had good relations with doctors." But he didn't wait for that to take effect. He immediately met individually with each hospital chief of staff and every trustee to listen to their concerns.

Physician trustee Mark Sherman acknowledges that, in contrast to his predecessor, Van Gorder was immediately accepted, but there was a caveat: "You're going to have a honeymoon period for the first six months or so, but then you have to back it up," Sherman says. "Chris has balanced confidentiality and transparency, and that has earned him trust. There is also a consistency to what he says. No matter where he goes or who he talks to, it's the same message—and all aspects of all choices are explained to everyone," he says.

Creating that transparency, a term used by virtually every Scripps executive to describe Van Gorder's leadership style, was his greatest challenge. "We were a secret organization," he explains. "The board was not given complete or open information and was therefore surprised when it all fell apart." Additionally, all six hospitals' financials and staffing information was lumped together, Panarisi says, making it impossible to know how individual hospitals were doing.

Income and margins were very grim when Van Gorder stepped in. The year 2001 saw a negative 2 percent operating margin and a $21 million loss. But by the end of fiscal 2002, the system had a 1.5 percent operating margin and a $17 million profit—a $38 million turnaround. The system reaffiliated with its largest medical group at Scripps Clinic along the way and in 2003 has a $67 million consolidated operating margin.

"He took a death spiral and transformed it, financially and spiritually," Kline says. "Initially there was a lot of suspicion and anger . . . Chris had to show that his interests served everyone's interests. He conveyed that . . . he leads by deed." And what were those deeds? Van Gorder says it has boiled down to restoring local hospital autonomy and listening to his hospital staff, particularly those "angry doctors."

Within his first three months, he decentralized operations control, returning direct authority over daily decisions at each hospital to a leadership team comprising its administrator, its head of nursing and its chief of staff. Finances were brought back to the local level as well, no longer lumped into one systemwide statement. All aspects of Project Scripps, including the systems of excellence, were dissolved.

"Each hospital's administration feels more in control," Sherman says. But at the same time, each hospital understands that it needs to balance its needs with those of the other hospitals. "It's like a family with five children deciding who gets what toys," Sherman says. "Chris asks 'If we could get this much money, how would you use it?' He asks physicians and administrators to prioritize how money will be used—it's a mutual decision-making process."

An Operations Council, comprising all the hospital administrators, and chaired on a rotating basis by one of them, meets monthly on their own to discuss those issues and more, and once a month they meet with the Executive Leadership Council, comprising all system senior management.

The Executive Council meets weekly, and once a quarter, both councils hold a full-day retreat. Van Gorder says such a system "delegates command and control where they belong and provides consistency and noncompetitiveness."

Physician Leadership Cabinet

But perhaps the most significant new structure Van Gorder has put in place is the Physician Leadership Cabinet (PLC), composed of the medical chief of staff, chief-of-staff-elect and the administrator at each hospital. A different nurse executive from one of the hospitals rotates through the council every six months as well. These elected hospital leaders meet with Van Gorder every month.

Although physicians had originally wanted their own board, Van Gorder said the system board would remain the only one, but added, "'Your informal power is bigger than that formal power. . . .' I have to respond to the elected physicians, and to this day, we have yet to not accept all recommendations made by the PLC."

In fact, six months after Van Gorder took the helm, the chiefs of staff at all five Scripps hospitals took out a full-page ad in the *San Diego Union-Tribune* expressing their support for their new CEO—the same group that had previously gone to that newspaper with a no-confidence vote.

"Chris knows how to deal with difficult doctors, how to develop consensus," Kline says. "The key is to seek first to understand, to hear their mission. Chris is absolutely transparent and direct." Kline adds that he always responds quickly to e-mails and overall is very "available and effective."

Sherman explains, "Just as communication is the most important part of a good marriage, concerns are directly addressed on both [management and physician] sides. Administration appreciates that and is willing to make changes based on what they learn, or if they can't do something, they explain why. Physicians greatly appreciate the truth, even if it's not what they want to hear."

As Scripps chief medical officer, Brent Eastman co-chairs the PLC with Van Gorder. He describes the role of the cabinet as both a direct advisory council to the CEO and an important communication vehicle back to hospital medical executive committees (MECs) and staff.

"There has been an extremely positive reaction to the PLC," Eastman says. "I hear [at MEC meetings], 'That ought to go to the PLC,' and I see there is recognition that it's a powerful tool. . . . It's unique to have all these people around the table."

Discussions range from malpractice insurance to the status of graduate medical education programs. Ad hoc committees have been formed from the PLC to look further into such specific issues as how to share the burden fairly for ED specialty coverage and disaster preparedness. Eastman tries to ensure that that agenda is generated by the PLC itself, asking members in advance for agenda items, but also leaving time at the end of meetings for open discussion.

"The PLC exemplifies how Chris wants to deal with physicians," Eastman says. "He has placed a lot of trust in [this] leadership to guide him. . . . Physicians have the majority vote on the PLC and by having chiefs-elect there, you also have younger people who will be around in the future."

Sherman adds that the impact of groups like the PLC extends throughout the system. "When physicians hear that their chiefs of staff feel like they're being dealt with fairly—and that wasn't the case five years ago—the impact trickles down. I see the same thing in middle managers in nursing who feel their supervisors have a definite purpose—the communication is there . . . and the PLC is at the root of physician satisfaction."

The PLC has assumed such importance that the board does not want to sign off on the strategic plan until it knows if the PLC has done so, Van Gorder says. What he calls "a godsend to the organization" has become the medical arm of strategy.

For example, physicians wanted a significant compensation hike for taking ED call and brought it up at the PLC. Van Gorder said he would accept whatever recommendation the cabinet came up with, but he explained that would necessitate cutting nurses' pay. The PLC went back to the ED call physicians and, ultimately, they settled for a lower raise, realizing the implications of their request. In essence, Van Gorder gave them all the information, and let them sit in his place.

Kline and Sherman were added to the board when Van Gorder became CEO, chosen in a method typical of Van Gorder's style, Panarisi says. All Scripps-affiliated physicians were invited to interview for the two new board slots in an open notice, but the notice made it clear that if elected, they were to serve as community representatives, not lobbyists for their hospitals. Panarisi says 50 doctors applied.

In addition to adding two more physicians, Panarisi says the board has made more changes on its own as a result of lessons learned. Meetings now rotate between the five hospitals, a "showing of the flag," as he calls it. A new independent auditor has been hired in connection with a restructuring of the audit committee, which Panarisi chairs. Most of all, the whole demeanor of board meetings has changed.

"We have opened up to more discussion—it was just reports given before," Panarisi says. "It's less formal [now], there's more interaction. The air is clearer. . . . We have confidence we are being told the truth."

Trustees sit in on various hospital MEC meetings to further their education on daily operations, and Panarisi says the board is "digging down further into performance than before" and is more savvy on ways to look for red flags in such areas as staff and physician recruitment and patient census.

What a Difference a CFO Makes

The board has had significant assistance through one of Van Gorder's most important other leadership changes. Richard Rothberger came in as the system's chief financial officer in the summer of 2001, and his leadership has been touted as much as Van Gorder's for his ability to make complex financial information clear and understandable. Rothberger went immediately to each hospital's administrator and MEC when he first arrived and explained their financial status straightforwardly.

"I think it helped build credibility to go and tell everyone how things were," Rothberger says. "I gave everyone a top-10 financial priorities list right away, and I promised to track those priorities and report back. I let [hospital administrators and MECs] know how much cash there was, what operations looked like, what was in the bank and what we needed to do to get a good bond rating to be able to borrow for more capital later."

Every month after the financials come in, each hospital management team meets with Rothberger to go over their numbers and see how they are proceeding with their annual operations plan and how they tie into the system's annual plan.

"The management teams understand why we need to do what we are doing," Rothberger says. "We are looking beyond our own careers and building a balance sheet that will help them in the years to come."

However, Scripps' boldest financial move so far to build a strong financial future has been to refuse capitation. With the dissolving of Project Scripps, the system cancelled all its capitated contracts, working now only on a fee-for-service basis—"a huge part of the turnaround," Van Gorder says, and a way to make revenues predictable.

"We were being short-paid in many areas," Rothberger says. "We set targets for how much we needed from each payer [and we told them], 'We will only take fee-for-service compensation from HMOs, and we will not take risk for services we do not provide.' We were willing to walk away from contracts if necessary. Our good name has continued to bring people in to see our doctors. There is no need to discount." Only one HMO refused to negotiate a new agreement.

Other than the Scripps Clinic, with which the health system reaffiliated in 2000, and which Scripps Health owns (except for the medical group contract within it, which is owned through an agreement with Scripps Foundation), all the system's affiliated physicians have total control over their own practices.

Rothberger says better revenue cycle management has contributed to the system's turnaround numbers as well. They reduced their accounts receivable days from 85 days to 68 days last year, bringing in $35 million in additional cash—a team effort, he maintains.

"Scripps has a lot of great people who were looking for a leader," Rothberger says. "Chris is able to make people better because of who he is. He works harder than anybody and has a passion to succeed . . . that spreads like wildfire."

"It boils down to leadership," Kline says. "He has managed a lot of hospitals, he has the internal discipline to not get spun out by disagreement. He promotes others, not himself. . . . It's a work of art to see him in action."

And he understands physicians. Van Gorder gives his father-in-law much credit for that, a doctor who advised him when he first began as an administrator on how to lead physicians.

"My father-in-law told me to be accessible, to listen and to follow up on all issues—that's the key to credibility," he says. "I learned a long time ago, I need to listen well. There are lots of people who know what must be done. I listen to the board, to physicians, administrators, employee groups, everyone. Really, if you're having good communication, one-on-one talks, it's easy to put the puzzle together."

Eastman believes such communication is critical. "The only way our health care system will survive is with a strong partnership between physicians and hospitals. With a mechanism like the PLC, we as physicians [can] come together and do the right thing if we are given the information and are being listened to. Physicians become [administration's] ally and partner."

PART FOUR

The Board Chair and the CEO

Side by Side: Communication Is Key to a Successful CEO–Board Chair Partnership

By Jan Greene

When Margaret Sabin became CEO of Marin General Hospital in Greenbrae, California, she knew she'd have her hands full. An ugly legal dispute over control of the hospital had been resolved shortly before she started there in early 2000, so she understood she'd be working in a fishbowl. When she decided the hospital should take a $9 million write-down (i.e., an adjustment to past financial statements) to institute a more conservative accounting stance on accounts receivable, she knew she might be inviting criticism. Most worrisome was that it might look as if she were publicly denouncing the board's financial oversight during the previous three years.

So she turned to businesswoman Etta Allen, who chairs the hospital board. "When I called her, I told her, 'Etta, I have terribly mixed feelings about this,'" Sabin recalls. "My gut tells me it's better for us to be as conservative as we can be, but I don't want to make it look like I'm reversing decisions of the last three years."

After having worked together for a year, Sabin and Allen forged a good working relationship, finding that they both like honesty, open

---

Jan Greene is a writer based in Alameda, California.

communication and brevity. Presented with Sabin's dilemma, Allen was supportive. "Etta said, 'You know, Margaret, it's a new day and it's a new way of looking at this, and we, the board, can support this.'"

Of course, that support didn't come overnight. In fact, the writedown issue was hashed out over five of the board's finance committee meetings and three meetings of the full board. "I give [Etta] credit for the board coming to the conclusion that it was the right thing to do, that it was just a different way of doing things with new leadership," Sabin says. And Allen gives the chief executive kudos, explaining that the board was able to resolve the issue in large part because of Sabin's "openness."

Sabin knows that getting that potentially explosive issue approved by the full board was a step-by-step process. And the first step was to nurture her relationship with Allen. "As health care gets more challenging . . . it really is critical that the CEO and board chair have the ability to connect," Sabin says.

Governance consultants and other successful CEO–board chair pairs agree. Because a chief executive and board leader may work closely together for just a couple of years, it's critical that the two establish good communication patterns early. "We decided right away we needed to meet every month," says Tom Strauss, CEO of Summa Health System in Akron, Ohio. "And we have discussions on an as-needed basis about what's happening." Those early conversations should also establish a partnership.

Openness and Honesty Are the Best Policies

"The best relationships I've seen are mutually supportive . . . where [the CEO and board chair] have a very open line of communication," says Mary Totten, president of Totten & Associates, Oak Park, Illinois. "The chief executive will use the board chair as a sounding board, looking for chances to think together and plan together."

Exactly how hospital leaders communicate can differ, however, depending on their management styles and personalities.

For instance, Sabin and Allen have face-to-face meetings when a particular issue needs their attention. But much of their work together is conducted during brief phone calls. "It doesn't have to consume a ton of time," says Sabin. "After five minutes Etta will say, 'OK, there we are. Have a nice day.' And I'll ask, 'How did we get that done so quickly?'"

Allen says she appreciates that Sabin is secure enough to share both good and bad news with her. "We both have this openness about us, so it's easy to pick up the phone and chat," she says. "We both express our opinions openly without any concern about [the potential to offend] each other."

Thaine Michie, board chair of Poudre Valley Health System in Fort Collins, Colorado, shares a similarly open relationship with the hospital's CEO, Rulon Stacey. "Rulon and I have a pact; there are no secrets between us," Michie says. "Rulon needs honest feedback because he might be doing something that upsets someone. He has to have someone he knows will tell him what's going on."

What the Board Chair Should Be Asking the CEO

1. How does our organization define quality, and what indicators should the board receive to monitor whether we're achieving our objectives?
2. Do we promote a "blameless culture" throughout the organization when it comes to reporting medical errors and near misses?
3. What are the organization's objectives for return on investment for our invested funds, and how can the board track them?
4. How satisfied are physicians with our strategic direction? What part do they play in helping us set that direction?
5. How do our corporate compliance policies and procedures function? What system do we have in place to ensure consistent and seamless compliance throughout the organization?
6. How sound is our organizational culture? What indicators should we use to measure our success in building a strong, cooperative, collaborative culture at every level?
7. What methods should we use to measure and report progress in achieving our strategic objectives and vision?
8. How does our audit committee function? What changes, if any, should be made in this area in light of the recent Enron developments?
9. How do we define a "healthy community," and what is our role in creating one? What indicators should we use to define success in this area?

Source: Larry W. Walker, The Walker Company, Lake Oswego, Oregon

The Partners' Profiles

Marin General Hospital, Greenbrae, California

One of 27 hospitals affiliated with Sacramento-based Sutter Health System; 235 beds

Margaret Sabin, CEO since July 2000; former CEO of two hospitals in Colorado

> Favorite thing about her partner: "She's got the ability to take a [board member] who has a head of steam about something and suddenly have him come around."

Etta Allen, board chair for five years; active in the community and owner of a heating and sheet metal company

> Favorite thing about her partner: "She's very inclusive of everyone in the organization. It's a pleasure to walk through the hallways with Margaret because she knows just about everyone by first name."

Summa Health System, Akron, Ohio

An integrated health care system, including two hospitals and a health plan

Tom Strauss, CEO since January 2000; took over from a CEO who held the position for 25 years

> Favorite thing about his partner: "We both have strong personalities. But she does a great job of holding back her comments until the board can consider an issue."

Ann Brennan, board chair since January 2000; longtime board member; active in the community

> Favorite thing about her partner: "He's an extremely likable person, and his values are the same as mine. He is truly dedicated to Summa Health System achieving world-class status."

Continued →

Poudre Valley Health System, Fort Collins, Colorado
A 235-bed hospital in a growing area; affiliations with many rural hospitals in nearby states

Rulon Stacey, president and CEO since 1997; the system's fifth CEO in four years

   Favorite thing about his partner: "He gives me a lot of autonomy."

Thaine Michie, board chair since 2000; retired electric utility executive

   Favorite thing about his partner: "We're both pretty open and honest people. I don't know anything he doesn't know, and he doesn't know anything I don't know."

St. Mary's/Duluth Clinic Health System, Duluth, Minnesota
A three-hospital Catholic system and a multispecialty clinic that merged in 1997

Peter Person, M.D., CEO since the 1997 merger; ran the clinic before the merger and took on the top job afterward

   Favorite thing about his partner: "I'm lucky to have someone who understands health care so well."

Sister Kathleen Hofer, board chair; St. Mary's CEO for 16 years before the merger

   Favorite thing about her partner: "There has been a complete openness with sharing information."

—J.G.

Stacey says he's careful to keep both Michie and the whole board aware of issues as they come up. He sends e-mails and faxes to board members 5 to 10 times a month "so they're not caught off guard," he explains.

Successful pairs report that they keep one another informed about everything they believe may be pertinent to the hospital's future. Smart CEOs use the board chair as an advisor with a valuable outside perspective and a community connection.

"I've seen the strongest and most effective CEOs willingly seek help from the board in general and view the board chair as the one person they can talk to and confide in," says Ed Kazemek, governance consultant and CEO of Accord Limited in Chicago. "That may be harder

---

Role Adjustment

If anyone really understands the difference between being a chief executive and being a board chair, it's Sister Kathleen Hofer. She's been in both roles as a result of a 1997 merger between St. Mary's Medical Center, Duluth, Minnesota, and the large, multispecialty Duluth Clinic. She went from a 16-year career as CEO of St. Mary's to serving as "active" board chair of the merged entity, which meant working nearly full-time to help the physician who ran the clinic take over as system chief executive.

The situation could have been very difficult for everyone. "You've got the potential for real fireworks," says Ed Kazemek, CEO of ACCORD, Ltd., Chicago, who works with the health system. "They both had to go through significant changes."

Sister Kathleen acknowledges the transition took a lot of effort. "I worked really hard at it," she says in retrospect. She used her strong belief in communication to work things out with the new CEO, Peter Person, M.D. "Initially, we worked together a lot as we were getting this new organization off the ground," she says. Now they meet for a couple of hours every Thursday morning.

As board chair, Sister Kathleen had to shift her focus from running the day-to-day operations of the hospital and "think a little more globally," she says. "I'm having to look at the much broader picture and at how decisions may have an impact on things over the long term."

Continued →

to do with members of your senior executive team. With the board chair, [CEOs] don't have to worry about information leaking out."

Some chief executives and board chairs see their partnership as more than a business arrangement. "We just nurtured it like any other relationship," says Ann Brennan, chair of the Summa Health System board of directors. She works with president and CEO Tom Strauss. "I will always count on him as a friend. And I will always be available to be a counselor or a sounding board."

Strauss and Brennan have a standing monthly meeting with each other before the system board meeting and talk more extensively on an as-needed basis. It helps that they like each other. "We enjoy each other's company," Strauss says. He even stayed with Brennan and

---

For his part, Dr. Person says he's benefited from Sister Kathleen's experience running the hospital. "We really have, over the last five years, developed a high degree of trust. We also know how each other thinks, which allows us to have open communication and prevents what I see so often, which is a lack of communication, which leads to distrust, which leads to dysfunction."

He's careful to be as open with information as possible to maintain trust. "If there's an area she's really interested in from an operational perspective, we talk as deeply as we need to rather than trying to compartmentalize ourselves in our roles," he says. "The more often you do that, the more confidence grows in decision making and trust about it, and the stronger ally I have in the board chair when we run into difficult issues."

At the same time, they have to be clear with the staff about who's running the operation. "If the culture in the past was for people to stop by her office, she has to refer them to me," Person says.

The pair has developed a joint vision for the hospital, which keeps physicians and employees from trying to use one against the other. "Because we were very committed to this common vision, there were no possibilities of an end run," Person says.

Kazemek has watched Dr. Person's and Sister Kathleen's relationship grow over five years. "From my vantage point, they have a really healthy board chair–CEO relationship. They are both very respectful of one another's opinions."

—J.G.

her husband in their Florida home when the two attended a governance educational conference. "That was very positive. I got to know her husband. He and I golfed together. I can't do that with Ann because she doesn't golf," he adds with a laugh.

Actually, doing business in a relaxed setting such as the ninth tee isn't a bad idea for CEOs and their board chairs, advises Errol Biggs, director of the Center for Health Administration, University of Colorado, Denver, and coauthor of *Practical Governance* (ACHE Management Series, 2001). "If the two happen to play golf, that works out very well," he says. "Or if they're having dinner together, it makes it easy to cover the key issues."

Communication is clearly one key to success. Another is knowing where the CEO's job ends and the board's responsibility begins.

Know Your Job

"One of the things that has made this [relationship] unique and workable is that we know our roles very well," says Marin board chair Allen. "The board carries out a policymaking role . . . but the day-to-day management of the hospital is certainly in Margaret's realm."

Board leaders say they often use common sense to decide how to draw the line between operational and strategic issues. "We talk about how we could improve our market share," says Summa's Ann Brennan. "Not the nuts and bolts of 'Are we going to cut four nurses here or do something with the laundry?'"

At St. Mary's Duluth (Minnesota) Clinic Health System, board chair Sister Kathleen Hofer says board members don't have too much trouble sticking with big-picture issues, in part because there's so much to know. "The best possible situation is to have the board as highly informed as it can possibly be," she says. "Some say they'll just get involved in operations. That's possible, but we can tell the difference. Besides, the lay people feel they're never as informed as they want to be. It's just too complex."

When board members start to wander into the CEO's domain, the results can be disastrous. "The worst position a CEO can get into is having a board get into micromanaging," says Sabin. "It can take a good CEO and neuter his or her ability [to run the hospital]. When that happens, the CEO really needs to go, because it's hard to bring that relationship back."

To avoid such a fate, organizations should strongly consider having roles and responsibilities in writing. Summa Health System, for instance, already has a job description for the chief executive. Now it has a governance committee of the board working on job descriptions for the board chair and trustees to help future members step into their roles more easily. The board also conducts a yearly self-assessment. "We're trying to move this whole self-governance to a more efficient process," says CEO Strauss.

Putting it all down in writing can help draw "that fine line between strategic leadership and operational leadership," notes Lake Oswego, Oregon, governance consultant Larry Walker, president of The Walker Company. "Often these things are taken for granted in smaller organizations. It's often handled in a very informal way. But a formal, written set of roles and responsibilities" would help prevent either the board or the CEO from encroaching on the other's responsibilities, he recommends.

The CEO can take the lead in defining those roles by providing the board with appropriate educational information. Such information should include top-level summaries of major issues, such as finance, compliance and strategic alliances. But it's important to strike the right balance—by providing too much detail, management runs the risk of either drawing trustees too far into operational issues or overwhelming them with information they simply won't have time to digest.

Walker says board members who have a lot of business expertise may ask operations-related questions, particularly if they're not being fed a regular diet of good strategic information. He defines that as "What does the board need to know to meet the challenges of the next few months?"

But information alone is not enough. Trustees must also be able to trust the information they're given, notes Van Johnson, CEO of the Sutter Health System in northern California, of which Marin General is an affiliate. When board members stray into micromanagement, "it's usually the result of discomfort with the CEO or with individuals who are providing the information," says Johnson, whose organization includes 27 hospitals, each with its own board, plus a number of system-level boards. "In some cases I get more concerned about the board becoming complacent and not asking the questions it needs to ask."

Errol Biggs suggests that boards should be asking the following kinds of questions:

- How will our organization survive in the evolving marketplace?
- What kinds of alliances or mergers should we consider?
- Are there joint ventures with physicians we should consider?
- How are we maintaining good relations with physicians, and how could we improve them?
- Do we have the right physician mix on staff?

Looking Ahead

After putting all this effort into forging a good working relationship, it can be hard on a CEO when it's time for the board chair to step down. But in most cases, consultants agree, it's important to let new blood in and reduce the chance that the chief executive and board chair will be seen as holding on to power for too long. That's fine with Poudre Valley's Michie. "It's not healthy for me to get too close to [CEO] Rulon [Stacey] and be chair for too long," he says. "Besides, after you've been chair, you're a better board member."

Occasionally, though, the rules need to be broken. For instance, the Marin General board decided to give Allen an extra three-year term as chairperson to maintain momentum on a touchy political situation that was finally improving just as her first term ended.

When the board chair changes, the CEO has to adjust to a new person and a new relationship. For instance, Margaret Sabin already knows who is in line to succeed Etta Allen and that they are likely to have more structured communication. "With that individual I will have a set meeting and an agenda, I can tell," says Sabin, "and I will have to modify myself." But that's part of her job, she acknowledges. "I don't think a CEO in this day and age can dictate how the board chair will relate to the CEO. The CEO has got to select a communication style that the board chair is most comfortable with."

Summa's Strauss reluctantly accepts that his partner, Ann Brennan, will step down at some point. "We're really just now beginning to hit the groove," he says. "The good news for us is that [former board chairs] stay involved. Our last board chair is still on the board and chairs the nominating committee. I still call upon him. I'm sure Ann will be there as well."

Synergy in Motion: The Board Chair and CEO Relationship

A High-Performance Organization Needs a Winning Team

By Elizabeth D. Becker-Reems

When you think about critical issues in health care, personal relationships usually aren't the first thing to spring to mind. But it is the "soft stuff" of relationships that can make the difference between a good health care organization and a great one. And the CEO–board chair relationship is one of the most significant.

Consider the situation at Mission St. Joseph's Health System (which was formed when Memorial Mission Hospital and St. Joseph's Hospital merged in 1998) in Asheville, North Carolina. Over the years, president and CEO Robert F. Burgin has seen the impact his relationship with various board chairs has had on board decisions and the organization's performance. Burgin recalls an instance early in his career when his chairman was president of a local technical college. As a new CEO, Burgin was eager to assert his authority and demonstrate his leadership ability. He saw his relationship with his chairman as necessary—but not critical, keeping him informed of critical decisions rather than directly involved in them.

Elizabeth D. Becker-Reems is the organization development consultant and Robert F. Burgin is president and CEO, Mission St. Joseph's Health System, Asheville, North Carolina.

"Although we don't have a significant seasonal swing in our patient volumes," Burgin says, "we did experience a major decline in Medicare reimbursement in the fall of 1984 as a result of the [initiation of] DRGs. We had just hired a large number of new graduates from the technical college, and money was tight. Management decided to lay off some of these new graduates.

"I didn't realize the implications of this move on more than the bottom line," Burgin continues. "I saw it as strictly a financial decision. Well, it was much more than that—and I received and asked for little input from our seasoned board chair or from other trustees. I didn't fully consider the impact on future graduates, who would be hesitant to come work for us. We didn't anticipate the staffing pressure that would occur in the heavy-volume months of January, February and March because of a decision I made in November. Instead of reducing cost, we incurred overtime and recruitment incentive expenses that could have been avoided if I had made a greater investment in my relationship with my chair and allowed myself to seek his advice and experience."

Get Started on the Right Foot

Not every board chair and CEO have the benefit of a long relationship before they start to work together. In 1986, the chair-elect at Memorial Mission withdrew at the last minute because of business pressures. A relatively new trustee, Garza Baldwin, head of the board's finance committee, was thrust into the position of chair. Baldwin worked in a small town about 30 miles from Asheville. He was not involved in the city's social life, and he and Burgin had had only limited contact before that time. Neither knew how their relationship would work, but both knew it was important.

At the same time, Burgin and his management team had determined that the hospital's emergency physicians' contract should be canceled because of performance problems. But Burgin wondered if he would have his board chair's support for this decision.

Fortunately, Baldwin turned out to be a strong chair, prepared to commit time and energy to his role and to his relationship with the CEO. He wanted to learn more about the intricacies of hospital operations and the medical staff's role in decision making. He also wanted to learn Burgin's strengths, weaknesses and personality. The two moved from a superficial relationship to one in which both felt comfortable giving and receiving advice and counsel. Baldwin and Burgin worked with the chief of staff to address potential medical staff fallout over the ED decision, and Burgin learned the value of receiving guidance from his chair.

Former Memorial Mission chair Bill Boswell says, "As your turn to become board chair approaches, you get a sense of whether you will be able to relate well with the CEO, and somehow that sense [influences] the rest of the relationship. If you believe your relationship will only be neutral, it is difficult to generate the commitment and energy to make it truly effective. It doesn't take long to form an impression, and it can be a blessing or a barrier to your relationship." Boswell believes that taking early ownership of the development, growth and maintenance of the relationship is the key. "Its effectiveness will have a long-term impact on the organization and on the CEO's future," he says.

Work from the Outside In

It's easier to start building the structural elements of a CEO-chair relationship before trying to develop a personal one. Burgin shares this story:

> I was somewhat hesitant in my initial meetings with the new chair, Bill Boswell, not fully sharing my thoughts and ideas. I respected him and believed he respected me, but we were relative strangers. Boswell was a strong manager and comfortable taking decisive leadership action. I knew that in a short time he would be evaluating my performance and would not hesitate to speak his mind. I had to ensure that his orientation and exposure to the hospital and to me was comprehensive. We started to structure more frequent communication and build a deeper understanding of our roles. In just a few months, I was as comfortable working with him as I had been with others whom I had known much longer.

The four basic strategies for working from the outside in require both parties to clarify roles, structure time together, share information and build a shared perspective.

Clarify Roles

Regardless of past experience or the orientation you receive as trustee or board chair, an in-depth exploration and agreement on roles is critical from the start. When the nurses go on strike, for example, whom should the newspaper call? When the ED doctors require a new contract, with whom do they negotiate? When the CEO is out of town, who makes critical decisions? Current Mission St. Joseph board chair Charles D. Owen III explains how that clarity helped him once when he first became chair:

> A community member contacted me about a potential racial discrimination problem at the hospital. This person wanted to discuss the situation with me and share details so that I could more fully understand what had happened. I felt a conflict because I represent the community but am also an advocate for the hospital. Fortunately, Bob [Burgin] and I had already spent time clarifying our roles, and I knew that I had to place this problem in his domain. That initial discussion kept me from making a mistake and from encroaching on what is more appropriately handled by the CEO and vice president for human resources.

To initiate a role clarification conversation, start by asking the CEO for a job description for the two of you. It will serve as a springboard for that in-depth discussion. Job descriptions give a good, but sparse, description of the chair's responsibilities; they do, however, serve as a catalyst and starting point for your discussion, and they can be changed. Part of clarifying the chair's role while enhancing the relationship-building process includes: grooming future board leaders; coaching, mentoring and evaluating the CEO; managing board composition; and managing policy, not operations.

The role clarification process sets the stage for how the chair and CEO will work together. The discussion should be enriched with the history, experience and perspectives that both bring to their role of the organization's leaders.

Owen describes a trip that he and Burgin took right before Owen became chair. "We went to a meeting for board chairs and CEOs. The meeting was excellent, and the networking was very beneficial to both Bob and me. But the benefits that stay with me were the out-of-meeting conversations that Bob and I had about our thoughts and perspectives on operations, policy and how we would work as a team.

"The forced togetherness of the trip—sitting side by side on the plane, meeting early for breakfast and sitting together in the evening to talk over the events of the day and to discuss how we would work together—was the beginning of a deep and trusting relationship."

Owen remembers that conversations about the conference moved into pertinent issues at Mission St. Joseph's. "Both Bob and I talked about our perspectives and learned where we agreed and where we differed. We weren't under the stress of needing an instant decision but were able to explore our differences and share the experiences that brought us to the beliefs we hold."

Structure Time Together

Both the CEO and the chair have a full life and responsibilities. Most likely, they both work from seven in the morning until seven in the evening and then have family and community responsibilities

---

Relationship Assessment

How can you tell if you have a high-performance relationship with your CEO? Ask yourself how many of the following statements apply to both of you.

1. We have taken time to get to know one another on a personal level.
2. We check on the relationship and occasionally ask each other how we are doing.
3. We take time to discuss difficult issues and are open about our thoughts and feelings.
4. We have attended educational programs together away from the hospital.
5. We accept each other's idiosyncrasies.
6. We are clear about our roles and responsibilities.
7. I routinely hear from the CEO several times a week and always in advance of a difficult or potentially explosive hospital issue.
8. We let each other know when we have done something that was "out of line."
9. We respect each other, including our differences, and our perspectives.
10. We forge ahead to resolve problems, even when the solutions are uncomfortable to implement.

after that. Neither has time to spare unless there are urgent issues to address. They could decide to spend time together only right before the monthly board meeting, making sure they plan the agenda and anticipate the group dynamics. But that is not the way to build a strong relationship.

How much time is the right amount? Early in the relationship it would be helpful to travel together to a meeting like the one that Owen and Burgin took. This forced time together helps ease barriers that exist just because neither person knows the other well. As an ongoing practice, it helps to meet a minimum of one to two hours every week. Take advantage of available time before or after a committee meeting for a quick update or input. This gives both the chair and the CEO time to discuss issues facing the hospital, time to build a shared perspective on those issues and time to develop strategies for addressing them. In addition, the two may find time to trade personal stories that will build a friendship, such as how they spent the weekend and a sports event they watched, or to update one another on personal matters, such as the great performance on the volleyball court by a son or daughter.

If you don't think you can invest all this time in your relationship, what can happen? For one thing, the CEO may start handling issues and developing strategies that you see as your responsibility or on which you can't agree. Burgin recalls past board chairs who were extremely busy in their full-time jobs and/or lived out of town. He took a much greater role in the organization because these chairs weren't available or involved.

If, as chair, you're not in touch or involved, you may discover that you are questioning your CEO's loyalty when you hear gossip in the community or are called by a physician who is bringing you information "for your own good." If you begin asking yourself, "What is my CEO up to?" you are experiencing the first signs of distrust, and it is important to begin spending more time together.

Share Information

One of the cornerstones of a high-performance relationship is sharing information. It could be as simple as letting the CEO know something that you overheard at a cocktail party or as complex as trying to describe why half the board will likely oppose the CEO's recommendation for an organizational strategy or direction. The more open and honest you are as chairman, the more likely the CEO will follow suit. It's also important to openly acknowledge your regret about an action you took or a mistake you made. This gives the CEO permission to admit mistakes and insecurities also.

Build a Shared Perspective

The board chair and the CEO need to develop a shared perspective about what constitutes a serious situation at the hospital. For instance, not having enough beds to accommodate inpatients can seem to be a boon—business is great; we are full! However, there may be long-term negative effects. For example, disgruntled physicians who can't admit their patients to the hospital may admit them elsewhere. Nursing staff who are burned out from the unrelenting stress of caring for more patients than they can reasonably handle may start to leave. These potential repercussions would not be apparent to someone outside health care. Building a shared understanding of the implications of situations, organizational systems and trends provides a framework for future discussions and decisions.

Working on the Inside

If you have addressed role clarity, set aside time to communicate, shared information and developed a shared perspective on what matters, you are ready to work on sustaining and deepening your relationship. You can feel your spirit or soul expand when you are involved in this deepening relationship. Those elements that reflect a deeper relationship include compassion, mutual growth, integrity and courage.

Compassion

Compassion is a heightened sensitivity and understanding of what other persons are experiencing, true empathy for their situation and caring. In a purely surface relationship, compassion may never be called upon or offered. It is one of the benefits of a strong relationship, and when it occurs, opens the door to deeper levels of communication and understanding.

Within the organization, the CEO has few, if any, people in whom he or she can truly confide. Most everyone has a vested interest in the outcome of a decision or situation. For example, at one time Burgin was agonizing over what to do about a key staff member whom he admired and respected, but who was unable to effectively function with peers and medical staff. Burgin needed a nonjudgmental ear, someone who could really listen and appreciate the importance of the decision that he was considering and the agony he was suffering. The board chair was available and really listened. He asked a few helpful questions that clarified the issue for Burgin. And that was all he had to do—just be there and listen.

Mutual Growth

As the dialogue between the chair and CEO deepens, both have enhanced opportunities to learn. The degree of information, background and experience that they share increases, as does their openness to new ideas and new perspectives.

For example, the local newspaper gave Mission St. Joseph's advance warning about a letter to the editor that was to appear. The letter was derogatory and signed by someone Burgin knew. His first reaction was to call the paper, explain the erroneous assumptions and give facts and figures to prove the errors. But having been in a similar situation before, the board chair suggested a different approach. He recommended arranging a face-to-face meeting with the letter writer, holding back any rebuttal and just opening up to the writer's concerns.

The chair explained why he thought this approach might work better and shared his prior experience. Burgin followed the advice and gained new insight from both the chair and the letter writer.

Integrity

One element of integrity is to be able to depend on congruence between someone's words and actions. If the CEO says he will be at a certain place at a certain time, he is there. If the chair says, "I will support you on this," he does not back down. No one easily forgives a breach of trust. For instance, if the CEO discovers that the board chair has openly derided him in the community, the two will never develop a deep relationship. If the chair discovers that the CEO is trying to manipulate the chair's opinion, trust will never deepen.

Over time, when both the chair and CEO recognize that they can depend on each other, the level of the relationship deepens.

Courage

Both the chair and the CEO need to feel comfortable giving each other constructive criticism. This means taking a chance that you are telling the other person something he or she may not enjoy hearing. But giving constructive feedback does not put a good relationship at risk; it deepens it.

CEO Burgin recalls the time when a small, but influential, group of physicians was determined to end his tenure with the organization. This was during the first year of the joint operating agreement between Mission Hospital and St. Joseph's. Once a full merger was completed, it would effectively eliminate the competition between the two hospitals and abolish the opportunities physicians had to play off one hospital against the other. Burgin's inclination was to dig in his heels and explain why he was not at fault for reducing their opportunities to play one hospital against another. The chair and chair-elect met individually with Burgin and suggested a different approach. He listened, took a deep breath and agreed to follow their advice. Burgin met with the physicians and accepted responsibility for any perceived problems that had occurred as a result of the joint operating agreement. He apologized for any of his behaviors that had made them feel he was ignoring their input, and he pledged to be more inclusive in all decisions about clinical operations. It took courage for the chair and chair-elect to be honest and persistent and for the CEO to listen to their criticism and change his behavior as a result.

Barriers to High-Performance Relationships

Three frequent, but not insurmountable, barriers to building a high-performance relationship are a prior poor relationship, sabotage and time.

Prior Poor Relationship

If you had difficulties, hard words or an outright bad relationship with the CEO before you became chair, you have some work to do to move the relationship to a new level. Although it's true that the CEO would not willingly allow the selection of a chair with whom he or she had previously had a bad relationship, circumstances may propel someone who does not have the CEO's full endorsement into that position. Slow and planned evolution to the chairmanship is not always possible.

One of the best techniques to resolve a prior poor relationship is to bring problems into the open and talk about them. Not talking about past problems allows them to fester and erode any progress you might otherwise make in building a relationship. But don't rehash problems to prove who was right. The best tactic is to acknowledge that problems occurred, that you regret they may have caused hard feelings and that you would like to put them behind you. This tactic can close the door on the past and give both the chair and CEO a transition to a new relationship.

Sabotage

A trustee, physician, someone in the community or an employee may seek to undermine the existing CEO or chair. Although this person may have a legitimate complaint, it doesn't help to go behind the other's back to resolve the problem. This can undermine the leadership and governance process. If both the chair and the CEO expect and require face-to-face problem solving, it is hard for anyone to succeed in underhanded behavior.

Former Mission St. Joseph's chair Jack Stevens remembers the power struggles that occurred during the merger between Memorial Mission and St. Joseph's. "During the period under the operating agreement and prior to the merger, I and other board members became aware of challenges to Bob Burgin's continued leadership from certain medical staff members and the St. Joseph's leadership. I could see the effort to undermine Bob and to change our perception of him as a highly competent leader. There were occasions when I and a select group had to meet with individuals and groups to hear their perspectives about the future of the organization and Burgin's continued role."

Stevens remembers that these discussions were uncomfortable, and that they were held without Burgin. "I made sure to keep Bob informed of what was happening, with whom we were meeting and what the tenor and outcome of the discussions were. I don't believe he ever felt that I was working behind his back. He was fully aware of the power struggle that was going on during that period."

Time

If the chair and CEO cannot spend time together, they will not be able to effectively build a relationship. When a CEO and board chair first meet to establish how they will communicate and how much time they need to spend together, it may be an eye-opener for both—but it is absolutely essential.

There is no question that not all CEOs and board chairs will have the type of relationship that creates performance at the level of championship teams. However, by investing time, clarifying roles and exhibiting compassion, integrity and courage, an improved relationship is possible. This relationship is critical—not just to the CEO and the chair, but to the entire organization and community.

PART FIVE

∞

Executive Compensation

CEO Measurement and Evaluation: The Three P's

By Claudia Wyatt-Johnson
and Edward Bancroft

Before you can determine how to compensate your CEO fairly, you must first measure and evaluate his or her performance. Three basic principles underlie a successful CEO evaluation—what we call "The Three *P's*":

- **Performance** expectations must be determined by board consensus.
- **Process** for the CEO evaluation must be clear, thoughtful and objective.
- **Politics** of the board-CEO relationship must be fully acknowledged and managed.

Performance

The first step in conducting a CEO evaluation is to decide what criteria you will use to determine how well the CEO is leading the

---

Claudia Wyatt-Johnson is a founding partner of Partners in Performance (PINP), Chicago. Edward Bancroft is a founding partner of Bancroft Consulting, Winnetka, Illinois.

organization. Measures of success flow from strategy—not just the easy-to-quantify measures that boards are often tempted to use, such as margin. The board and CEO should first develop a long- and short-term organizational strategy upon which all agree and which all thoroughly understand. A designated group of trustees and key leaders should meet to determine this strategy and present it to the full board.

The best performance measures are integrated and comprehensive. Seen together, they tell a story about the organization's values and goals. Measures in a health care setting include financial benchmarks, such as net income or margin, and quality-of-care metrics (developed with the medical staff), such as readmission and postsurgical infection rates. Patient and employee satisfaction measures and hospital–medical staff relations are often used to round out the CEO "scorecard."

But hard measures are only one part of the equation. What often derails executives is not the actual results, but the actions and behaviors—such as strategic thinking or skills in building community relationships—needed to achieve those results. The board must be able to articulate the actions and behaviors it expects and clearly communicate them to the CEO.

Christopher Bennett, board chair of Woodstock, Illinois-based Centegra Health System, which comprises two hospitals, a psychiatric facility and outpatient clinics, says, "A full 40 percent of [our] CEO's evaluation is based on building relationships with the broad community, the medical community, the board and the staff."

Process

CEO evaluation methodology must be developed with a high degree of board involvement and meet the needs of both the board and CEO. Often, the board is not actively engaged in the process; the CEO generates his or her own evaluation criteria—a practice which, for obvious reasons, is fundamentally flawed.

"It must begin with a clear agreement on [board-CEO] authority," Bennett explains. "We developed a very specific authority matrix to set a firm foundation for our goal-setting and evaluation." An effective process includes a manageable method of setting expectations, gathering observations from staff and trustees and delivering timely feedback to the CEO.

The best evaluation methods are two-way, allowing the board and CEO regular opportunities to both recognize and improve performance. At Centegra, the board chair, vice chair and CEO meet weekly, either in person or by phone, to review progress.

Politics

The relationship between the CEO and board is complex and unique to each organization. Internal board relationships and individual and collective board-CEO relationships can pose the greatest challenges to achieving fair performance reviews.

Often close friendships exist between trustees and the CEO that can cloud objective judgment. If a board member was introduced originally to the group by the CEO, acting independently can be difficult.

Bennett explains how the Centegra board addressed this issue: "We shortened board member terms and set explicit criteria for board membership to minimize the 'friendship criteria.'"

In addition, performance measures should be compared with local and national norms. This takes the discussion away from the parties at hand and makes it more objective.

"The board and the CEO must look at the measures and decisions made on the basis of those measures aggressively if they are to stand up to scrutiny," Bennett advises.

Often, CEOs are chosen because they are aggressive and independent. These characteristics can potentially lead the CEO to seek autonomy or dominance rather than partnership with the board. To guard against this, the board must assert itself. It must stand up for the direction it has set and effectively represent its constituencies, whether they be stockholders or members of the community at large.

Steps to Effective CEO Review

To avoid backtracking and stumbles throughout the evaluation, the board should follow these steps:

- Set the direction for the review process: This can be done through interviews or group discussion with board members and

the CEO. The main focus of these discussions is to explore how reviews were conducted in the past and then set goals for the new, improved process. The evaluation process must serve as the vehicle to ensure the CEO is taking the organization in the right direction.
- Educate the board and CEO: Board members and the CEO can learn about prevailing evaluation practices through reading or presentations. Staying on top of evaluation best practices requires ongoing, consistent education planning by key board committees and staff.
- Decide on performance criteria, a two-step process: First, working with the CEO, the board must develop a mission, vision and values for the organization. This becomes the foundation for a timed business strategy that key board and staff members who are expert in their areas can then use to develop annual goals and measures for the organization. These goals and measures become the "what" of CEO expectations.

Secondly, the board decides on the competencies they expect the CEO to demonstrate. These competencies must be fundamental to achieving the organization's mission and become part of the expectations that are communicated explicitly to the CEO. They form the "how" of performance criteria.

- Schedule steps in the review process: The board should work through these steps on their annual calendar, beginning with an explicit agreement among all participants on what the standards should be. The board will want to consider using input from the CEO's direct reports, other key constituencies (especially physicians in the system) as well as individual trustees. The goal here is to get a comprehensive and accurate picture of the CEO's performance. The schedule should also include regular updates on progress made toward meeting goals during the year.
- Make decisions about compensation: The results of the review, which are documented on a performance form, will drive the compensation decision. The key here is to make a market and performance-based decision that reinforces messages of fairness and a culture of achievement.

Politics Revisited

Although the steps detailed above seem straightforward and logical, what often derails the evaluation's success is the third *"P"*—politics. There are several ways to manage politics and give boards and their CEOs a greater chance of success.

First, go slowly and be sure everyone has an opportunity to be involved. This is achieved by thoughtfully using the committee structure and effective methods to survey board members about their assessment of the CEO and the process as a whole. We recently worked with an organization that had conducted an organizational compensation review without the full board's involvement. (Intermediate Sanctions hold the board responsible for ensuring that compensation for *all* "disqualified" executives is reasonable.) Caught off guard when it came time for the next review, board members felt they needed to get involved in every small detail. That's probably not the best use of the group's time, but it was the only way to restore trust.

Using an objective third party can help get this aspect right. A consultant who has the trust of both the board and the CEO can often ask the uncomfortable questions that need to be asked if the process is to be jointly owned and, by doing so, can speed up the process at the same time.

Finally, naming the "moose on the table" is an important group practice. Often, the most challenging issues involve personalities and relationships. If there is an uncomfortable issue that is blocking progress, it is often avoided simply because it is uncomfortable. Even though everyone can see the moose, it is not discussed, so it sits and blocks progress and erodes trust for the future. "Types of moose" might include: apparent conflicts of interest; a CEO's consistent failure to supply the right information to the board; or a nonperforming board member, who may block effective dialogue.

Talking through and confronting such big and uncomfortable issues will contribute to the long-term health of the organization and an effective review process.

By working through these steps and avoiding pitfalls, the board can effectively meet one of its most important responsibilities—evaluating the CEO. It is one critical step toward the elusive goal of good governance.

Calibrating Executive Compensation

By Claudia Wyatt-Johnson
and Christopher J. Bennett

The American media are in a feeding frenzy over executive compensation. Hardly a day passes without a major publication or network revealing yet another executive fat cat who has pilfered the corporate coffers, thrown lavish parties at the shareholders' expense or cooked the books to line his pockets. The list grows each week: Enron, WorldCom, Tyco, HealthSouth. And with HealthSouth, the battle is drawing closer and closer to U.S. health systems.

If American for-profit corporations are under the microscope of executive compensation muckrakers, how long will it be before they turn their attention to the not-for-profit health care sector? Nearly everyone in government and the media is seeking to assign blame for the "skyrocketing cost of health care." Are there fat cats to be found there too? Can we blame them for soaring costs? Internal Revenue Service Form 990 makes the level and content of executive pay in the not-for-profit world a matter of public record. Anyone

---

Claudia Wyatt-Johnson is a founding partner of Partners In Performance (PINP), Chicago. Christopher J. Bennett is board chair of Centegra Health System, Woodstock, Illinois.

with a minimal level of curiosity and research ability can become the next whistle-blower.

Over the last 20 years or so, the not-for-profit health system has been striving to become more like the for-profit corporation. The languages of marketing and finance are spoken everywhere. Mergers and acquisitions are commonplace. So, too, have executive compensation levels and perks increased to resemble their corporate counterparts. Incentive compensation, virtually unknown in the health care field 20 years ago, is now offered to more than 90 percent of major medical center CEOs. Perquisites and supplemental executive retirement plans have proliferated. Although stock options account for much of corporate executives' remuneration, even without those, total compensation in not-for-profit health systems has risen dramatically.

Unlike their corporate counterparts, the volunteer boards of hospitals and health systems typically are not peer CEOs or industry executives with a working knowledge of what constitutes the amount and content of typical executive compensation programs over which they have oversight. For the most part, trustees who serve at urban medical centers are physicians or corporate executives without administrative experience in a health system. Suburban and rural trustees are typically physicians, individual entrepreneurs, community leaders or managers in smaller enterprises. And they are volunteers—unprepared and unrewarded for the level of oversight required by Intermediate Sanctions (see "What Trustees Should Know about Intermediate Sanctions," page 123) and community expectations.

So, what can a trustee do to avoid the scrutiny and public condemnation facing corporate boards? How can trustees ensure that executive compensation levels are competitive but not excessive? How careful must trustees be about Intermediate Sanctions? How can they ensure that executive compensation programs are serving the best interests of the hospital's constituents?

Fortunately, the process is not rocket science. Responsible trustees (i.e., the executive committee) must develop a working understanding of the process, norms, terms and regulatory requirements of executive compensation in a not-for-profit health system so that they can lead those who are compensated (e.g., management). And, while perceptions of "competitive" and "overpaid" vary depending on one's perspective, there are some straightforward steps to help ensure that executive compensation serves your medical center well.

What Trustees Should Know about Intermediate Sanctions

By Bonita L. Hatchett

Intermediate sanctions are excise taxes imposed by the Internal Revenue Code on "disqualified" managers who receive compensation disproportionate to the value of their services on behalf of a tax-exempt organization. (Potential beneficiaries of lucrative executive compensation arrangements sponsored by exempt organizations are considered "disqualified persons" for intermediate sanctions purposes.) The intermediate sanction rules are therefore designed to prevent disqualified persons from receiving unreasonable compensation. Members of an exempt organization's board are often deemed as "organization managers," and are also at risk for the imposition of the excise tax by virtue of approving compensation for their CEOs.

Trustees must consider the effect that their executive compensation arrangement will have on the value of an executive's total compensation package, and whether the provision of additional benefits will render the individual's overall compensation unreasonable. A "reasonableness" determination should consider the factors that are relevant to the safe harbor discussed below and should also take into account the type, quality and quantity of services provided by the executive on behalf of the exempt organization. Incentive-based compensation, the payment of which is contingent on attainment of predetermined goals, is also encouraged by the IRS and attorneys as long as the compensation is in proportion to the value of the services performed.

Two safe harbors exist for the sole purpose of providing relief from the punitive effects of intermediate sanctions. Trustees should use one of these two safe harbors in order to avoid the excise tax.

Rebuttable Presumption Safe Harbor

Under the rebuttable presumption safe harbor, compensation is deemed reasonable if certain requirements are met. First, the compensation arrangement must be approved by the board under circumstances wherein no trustee would be acting under a conflict of interest.

Continued →

Second, the board must obtain and rely upon comparable data prior to determining compensation. This could include engaging a professional to analyze data from similar exempt organizations regarding the value and type of compensatory arrangements provided to peers, reliance on compensation surveys prepared by independent firms, written offers of employment to executives from similar institutions and other relevant information.

Third, the board is required to document the basis for its compensation determination concurrently with making its reasonableness determination.

Reasoned Written Opinion Safe Harbor

The board may also rely upon the reasoned written opinion of a professional possessing expertise relevant to compensation. Trustees may be successful in avoiding the excise tax even if the professional's opinion is later determined to be incorrect, as long as the analysis was based upon relevant information and analysis of the proper legal considerations. Individuals qualified to issue these opinions include lawyers, certified public accountants and investment valuation experts.

The intermediate sanctions excise tax imposed upon a disqualified person is 25 percent of the excess benefit received, which may be increased to include an additional 200 percent excise tax if the transaction is not corrected within the taxable period. The CEO may also be assessed an excise tax equal to 10 percent of the excess benefit unless an exception applies.

Intermediate sanctions present a challenge to the boards of exempt organizations when designing competitive executive compensation arrangements, but they are a regulatory hurdle that can be cleared.

Bonita L. Hatchett, J.D., is a member of the national law firm of Bell, Boyd & Lloyd LLC, Chicago.

Surfing Lake Wobegon—The Typical Process of Design and Review

The standard procedure for designing and reviewing executive compensation in a not-for-profit health system is similar to that for a for-profit corporation. Usually, a member of the executive team hires an executive compensation consultant to advise on compensation levels and design for the executive team. Occasionally, the board is involved in the consultant selection process. All too frequently, however, it is not.

Often, these consultants are from the same firms currently being scrutinized for advising corporate executives. Frequently, these firms have large contracts and annuity relationships to advise the health system on pensions and benefits. This may be a conflict because compensation analysis is not necessarily an objective process. In a recent survey of corporate governance, cited in the September 2003, issue of *The Economist,* excessive executive compensation levels were named as the top governance concern, replacing auditor independence, trustees' previous greatest concern. The two issues can merge in the executive compensation review and recommendation process.

The consultant researches published survey data of peer institutions, which are generally identified by net patient revenue. In a report that generally exceeds 20 pages with sophisticated graphs and charts, the consultant will define "competitive" and then typically advise the institution to target total compensation at the 60th or 75th percentile or above. After all, how can any institution attract superior talent with only average pay?

That's where the "Lake Wobegon Effect" takes over. As in Garrison Keillor's mythical town where "all the children are above average," all the executives being reviewed are also above average or "they wouldn't be here." Therefore, the executives in question must be paid above average as well—and not just a little. The 75th percentile has assumed mythical proportions. Executive compensation levels in health care—as in industry—continue to spiral upward. And, no well-intentioned trustee wants the stigma of relegating leadership to average status no matter how uncomfortable he or she is with the logic of the pay-setting process.

If the laws of supply and demand applied, in many instances executive compensation levels would not be increasing. In fact, they might be decreasing as ongoing merger and acquisition activity and downsizing reduce the supply and scope of executive positions. The nature of pay makes it impossible to create a single formula or offer a single answer as to what is competitive and what constitutes "too much." The answer may lie in establishing a process and protocol that gives trustees the information and tools they need to make an appropriate decision.

How Centegra Took Charge of the Process

After assuming the role of board chair for Centegra Health System, based in Woodstock, Illinois, Chris Bennett met with the executive committee to review the current CEO's total compensation package and the system's performance review process.

The committee felt strongly that the CEO performance evaluation process required updating and enhancement. They wanted to establish goals and objectives, and they wanted to tie compensation to achievements without the burden of a complex or cumbersome system. The committee wanted a competitive compensation package to include salary, incentives, benefits and perquisites, and it was interested in obtaining comparable data on a national, regional and local basis.

Feedback on CEO performance was solicited from the board, the medical staff and the senior vice presidents through three separate questionnaires designed by—and for—each group. Once completed, the questionnaires were mailed directly to the outside consultant to be tabulated, ensuring confidentiality.

The committee then developed an incentive plan to reward effective leadership in meeting key objectives, including the system's mission and vision. There were four objectives:

- Financial Performance
- Strategic Performance and Key Relationships (i.e., evaluations by the board, medical staff, executive team and associates [i.e., employees])
- Patient Satisfaction (measured by Press Ganey)
- System Growth and Stability (i.e., new programs and/or facilities, negotiations with other systems, system image and development of a succession plan)

Once the evaluation process was in place, the committee reviewed comparable total compensation data for systems of similar type and size. The committee reviewed both national and regional survey data as well as IRS Form 990 information on their local competitors.

The committee determined a desired competitive compensation position based on the individual circumstances of Centegra and the findings of the analysis. Incentive targets were set to reflect threshold, target and maximum performance levels for each of the four annual objectives.

At the conclusion of the fiscal year, performance related to the four objectives was reviewed. That review led directly to a decision on annual incentive and Supplemental Executive Retirement Program (SERP). Base salary was also reviewed, as were the other elements of total compensation.

The committee and the board are extremely happy with the process and approach to measurement. Minor changes and adjustments will be made each year to keep the plan current.

A Ten-Step Process

Based on its experience, the Centegra board offers the following advice for a 10-step process for determining the CEO compensation package:

Step one: Staff the executive committee with tough, thick-skinned trustees who are critical thinkers and do not bow to pressure. Executive compensation is a key process that should be closely linked to the strategic planning process. The committee should comprise four or five members, at least one of whom should be a physician so that he or she can reflect the perspectives of the medical staff to the board and communicate the board's perspective to the medical staff. The committee should also have some overlap with the board's human resources committee because compensation is compensation, regardless of whether it applies to executives, nurses or therapists, and the institution's overall philosophy should be the same.

Step two: Hire an advisor who reports directly to the committee. This individual—or firm—should not have other substantial contracts with the medical center, and certainly no large, annuity-based financial relationship that might compromise objectivity. The primary purpose of this advisor is to educate the committee so that members can make sound, informed decisions.

Step three: Focus solely on the CEO. The board may review other executive pay levels, but the CEO should determine their compensation. Trustees frequently attempt to make decisions on compensation for the entire executive team at once. The rest of the executive team is the CEO's responsibility, and board interference undermines this role. However, the board should know what is being paid to members of the team—in base salary, incentives and other elements of total compensation, to ensure that no excess benefit transactions take place.

Step four: Work with the advisor to define the competitive market for senior executives. This is the basis for defining competitive compensation levels. Perhaps the most frequently stated—and poorly understood—aspect of the compensation-setting process is the definition of "competitive compensation." The dictionary defines it as "good or better than comparable circumstances." The committee must clarify and define comparable hospitals or health systems. These organizations should represent likely sources for senior executive recruitment. It is essential that these organizations have roughly similar gross revenues, since gross revenues are better indicators of the scope of services provided, while net revenues are more indicative of payer mix. The market for CEOs is national, so while trustees may want to focus on the medical center down the road or the system across town, the local scene is not representative of the competitive landscape.

Step five: Define all the elements of the total compensation package—and research competitive practices on all of them. The CEO's total compensation will typically include:

1. Base salary—the largest single element of total executive compensation.
2. Annual incentive—reward for meeting or exceeding preestablished objectives, representing above-average performance for the year.
3. Benefits—includes the health, disability and retirement package available to all staff at the institution.
4. Perquisites—best offered as a fixed amount allowance from which the executive can select any relevant items.

5. SERP—a supplemental executive retirement program to help augment post-retirement income over the current cap on "qualified" compensation. There is a growing trend to attach awards under these nonqualified plans to the attainment of performance objectives.
6. Executive benefits—organizations often offer a higher level of disability income or life insurance to senior executives to reflect their higher standard of living.

Step six: Review competitive compensation information from a published survey database and from an analysis of IRS Form 990s from select institutions. The combination of information from large, published surveys, as well as from a sample of specific organizations (presented separately) offers both an overview and an in-depth view of actual total compensation practices and levels. Form 990 separates total compensation reporting into cash compensation (base salary plus annual incentive), benefits and perquisites.

Step seven: Require that findings be presented in a brief, focused format in layman's terms. The report should depict the 25th, 50th and 75th percentiles for all the major elements of total compensation. After review and discussion of the content, committee members should have a strong sense of the competitive landscape. Actual pay levels for CEOs of comparable institutions can vary by 100 percent or more based upon individual circumstances, including tenure, financial viability, organizational complexity and how aggressive an executive is in pushing for additional compensation.

Step eight: Determine the organization's desired competitive position on each of the six elements of total compensation and on an overall basis. There is logic to targeting the base salary of a new CEO at the 25th percentile or below since he or she is in a learning mode and, presumably, will grow into the job. Base salary can be increased each year as (and if) that growth occurs. A good rule of thumb is to keep those elements of total compensation that are not related to performance and outcome at—or below—the competition. Those elements that are related to performance, such as an annual incentive, should be very generous when the CEO's performance is well above the majority of his or her peers.

Step nine: Develop an approach to measure the CEO's performance. A pay-for-performance approach requires a straightforward and objective process to measure performance. The annual incentive plan should be based on three to four key objectives that reflect a not-for-profit system or hospital CEO's broad and complex responsibilities. Objectives should include financial, patient satisfaction and strategic performance, and evaluators should form a "360-degree" feedback process that includes the board, the medical staff, employees and patients. A generous—and expensive—SERP should also reflect executive performance, rather than being constructed as an entitlement.

Step ten: Review and improve the program each year to reflect changes in the system's priorities and the environment.

Conclusion

The New Year is an ideal time for trustees to resolve to become informed overseers of executive compensation. After the first year's steep learning curve, subsequent compensation updates can be completed more easily. As new members rotate onto the compensation committee, they might begin their tenure with a two-hour crash course to bring them up-to-speed on the issue and to ensure continuity.

Some food for thought: Over our 25 years or more of consulting, we have observed that the most effective and successful CEOs are generally far less concerned about their own personal fortunes, while those who are less effective frequently seem obsessed with adding more and more to their compensation packages. Exceptional executives are attracted by the challenge of health care leadership and are motivated by achievement. Running a medical center is a challenging and demanding role, and it deserves to be well-compensated. But, excessive compensation is not consistent with the mission and vision of a not-for-profit health system. Dissension between the trustees and the CEO over compensation is often a symptom—not a cause—of a larger problem. Well-versed trustees can move quickly beyond compensation decisions to the really important task of helping to guide a successful hospital or health care system.

Avoiding Scandal: Recommended Practices for Board Executive Compensation Committees

By Michael W. Peregrine, Ralph E. DeJong and Timothy J. Cotter

Board members who are responsible for executive compensation are now in the hot seat as a result of the many corporate scandals in both the for-profit and not-for-profit sectors that have involved executive pay. In the wake of these scandals, regulatory agencies, legislators and courts have focused their attention on how governing boards may or may not have effectively reviewed executive compensation arrangements.

Such scrutiny has been accompanied by calls for reform in both for-profit and not-for-profit organizations. Legislative proposals, as well as regulatory and enforcement initiatives, are calling for independent board compensation committees to develop, review, approve and monitor executive compensation arrangements. To stay current with good governance practices, boards of not-for-profit organizations should move toward adopting a "best practices" standard developed

---

Michael W. Peregrine is a partner in the law firm of McDermott Will & Emery, L.L.P., Chicago. Ralph E. DeJong is a partner in McDermott Will & Emery, L.L.P., Chicago. Timothy J. Cotter is managing director, Sullivan, Cotter & Associates, Detroit.

by public policy groups (e.g., the Business Roundtable), professional associations (e.g., the American Bar Association) and major corporations (e.g., General Electric) for the use of an independent board-level compensation committee. This action begins with the organization's compensation philosophy statement.

Compensation Philosophy Statement

A well-formulated compensation philosophy statement (see "Sample Executive Compensation Philosophy" on pages 133–135) will eliminate the need to reinvent a policy each year. Beyond the sheer efficacy of having a starting point when determining executive compensation, a clear compensation philosophy statement can also:

- Articulate the organization's long-term policy on executive compensation.
- Support the organization's charitable purposes.
- Promote greater consistency from year to year regarding executive compensation.
- Mandate a process that qualifies for the strongest legal protection available under the IRS intermediate sanctions rules.

Once the board has determined that it should shape or revise its compensation philosophy, the next consideration is the scope and content of the statement. The recommended best practice is to craft a philosophy statement that reflects the following guiding principles:

- All elements of executive compensation and benefits and of the compensation process should be controlled by the compensation committee.
- The full board should approve the philosophy and strategy underlying executive compensation and receive regular reports on the extent to which the program adheres to these guidelines.
- Trustees who serve on the compensation committee, together with their lawyers and consultants, must be independent and not have more than a minimal conflict of interest relative to the compensation being reviewed, the executives whose compensation is being reviewed or any products or services being considered (e.g., insurance, estate planning, tax shelters).

Sample Executive Compensation Philosophy

Exempt Organization ("Exempt") recognizes that it needs strong and effective executive leadership to achieve its mission and to serve its community effectively.

1. The board's compensation committee shall be responsible for the review and approval of all forms of compensation and benefits provided to executives of Exempt (i.e., those employees whose base salary exceeds the highest nonexecutive pay grade [specify that grade]).
2. To assist in recruiting and retaining the quality of leadership necessary, Exempt will target the total compensation program for senior management at the "X" percentile of total compensation offered by organizations with which Exempt typically competes for executive talent, including:
   - Comparably sized health care organizations
   - Peer health care organizations (as defined by proximity, size and market conditions) in the [specify city, metropolitan area or region in which Exempt is located] geographic area.
3. When Exempt's performance is at the upper end of the scale (i.e., beyond the "X" percentile of similar organizations), the executive compensation program will move compensation levels to a similar percentile of total compensation to reward Exempt executives for this top-level performance.
4. Base salaries will be set within the range from the market [specify target numbers for this range] percentiles of base salaries for comparable positions at similarly situated organizations. The competitiveness of executives' base salaries is reviewed on an annual basis, and adjustments are made when market conditions warrant and financial performance allows. The size of the adjustment will be based on the executive's experience, performance and contribution to Exempt's performance, as well as on the competitiveness of the executive's salary within the marketplace.
5. Except in unusual circumstances, and as approved by the compensation committee (acting upon the CEO's recommendation for all executive salaries other than his or her own), base salaries will not exceed the market [specify target number] percentile of base salaries. This recognizes the fact that

Continued →

Exempt's executive total compensation program emphasizes and rewards outstanding performance through incentive award opportunities.

6. Exempt will use annual incentives, long-term incentives or both to enhance its ability to achieve its mission and its executive compensation objectives. The payment of an incentive award to any executive is completely contingent on that executive achieving pre-established performance targets.

7. Annual incentive target and maximum opportunities for Exempt executives will approximate the market [specify target number] percentile of target and maximum award levels for comparable positions at similarly situated organizations. Annual target and maximum opportunities will be reviewed on an annual basis and adjusted prospectively as necessary. Up to [specify number] performance measures will be used in Exempt's annual incentive plan and will include, at a minimum, an overall financial performance indicator and a patient satisfaction or other quality-of-care indicator. Annual incentive plan measures and performance levels will be presented to the compensation committee for review and approval before the beginning of each cycle.

8. Exempt's long-term incentive compensation plan will consist of discrete [specify period] year performance periods (i.e., when cycle one is completed, cycle two will begin) and is intended to focus attention on strategic objectives and serve as an executive retention device.

   Annual long-term incentive target and maximum opportunities will approximate the market [specify target number] percentile of target and maximum awards levels for comparable positions at similarly situated organizations so that, when maximum annual and long-term incentives are paid, total direct compensation approximates the market [specify target number] percentile of total direct compensation.

   Long-term incentive awards will be based on the base salaries in effect at the beginning of the performance cycle and will be paid as lump sums at the end of each three-year performance period. Plan measures and performance levels will be presented to the compensation committee for review and approval before the beginning of each cycle.

Continued →

> 9. Exempt also provides, as part of its competitive compensation package, certain standard benefits, supplemental benefits and perquisites. These programs are designed to support the executives in their professional roles and to address benefit limitations imposed by tax law rules affecting the qualified retirement plan design.
> 10. Exempt recognizes its responsibility to ensure that its executive compensation program is appropriate in view of its mission and tax-exempt status and that its compensation and benefits are reasonable and not excessive. To that end, Exempt will review and approve all forms of executive compensation and benefits in a manner necessary to qualify for the "rebuttable presumption of reasonableness" under the intermediate sanctions rules of Section 4958 of the Internal Revenue Code.
> 11. The compensation committee shall ensure that all elements of compensation and benefits provided to executives of Exempt are disclosed (a) to the full board on a regular basis and (b) on Exempt's annual IRS Form 990 annual return to the extent required by law.

- Total executive compensation levels should be reasonably linked to the organization's charitable purposes. This requires going beyond financial performance measures.
- Compensation arrangements should be comparable to similar organizations and jobs. The actual market positions should be linked to each executive's contributions toward achieving the organization's charitable purposes.
- All elements of the executive compensation program should be reviewed and approved annually by the compensation committee to ensure that its work continues to qualify under the intermediate sanctions rules.
- Compensation arrangements should be designed so that they can be easily explained to, and understood by, individuals with a basic business background.
- Full disclosure of the executive compensation and benefits program must be made as legally required on the IRS Tax Form 990, and the program should be structured so that full disclosure can

be made to the organization's stakeholders without embarrassment to the organization or executives.
- A well-formulated philosophy statement typically will be three or four pages and will delineate guiding principles by which reasonable compensation consistent with the organization's mission will be determined by independent board members.

The Compensation Committee's Structure and Function

An important issue for committee organization is whether the committee is controlled by (good) or fully composed of (even better) independent directors. While there may be practical factors that could affect this issue (such as the availability of qualified directors), corporate responsibility strongly suggests having a fully independent committee. Trustees who have more than a minimal interest in the compensation process or its outcome should not participate.

Qualifications. It's important to emphasize that there is no absolute requirement that applies to, or that fits, all organizations. The individual organization should develop a definition of independence that best serves its particular governance needs, taking into consideration the above factors and state and federal laws on this delicate topic.

In addition to independence, compensation committee members should have the following:

- Time—able to commit the time necessary to fulfill the committee's duties.
- Savvy—able to understand and work with sophisticated compensation concepts, options, costs, risks and implications.
- Mission Support—able to make executive compensation decisions that ensure that the needs of the organization and its stakeholders, as well as its charitable purposes, are met.
- Balance—able to weigh the potentially competing objectives of linking compensation to performance, retaining high-performing executives, minimizing adverse community and employee reaction and ensuring that the organization's charitable mission is maintained.

- Healthy Skepticism—able to critically review the performance and market practice data that are presented to the committee and apply the relevant information fairly.
- Outspoken—able to present firmly his or her viewpoints to fellow committee members (as well as to the full board), and clearly explain the organization's executive compensation rationale to internal and external groups.

An additional consideration is committee membership. To ensure that the above qualifications are met (including the independence of committee members), the board should give particular attention to appointing qualified committee members and have a rotation process through the use of term limits.

For boards that want to adopt best practices, we strongly recommend establishing a written charter that describes specific committee duties. These duties should include: (a) establishing a compensation philosophy; (b) identifying procedures for committee functions; (c) establishing performance objectives and evaluating performance; (d) conducting/assisting in succession planning; (e) assuring that executive compensation is administered consistently according to the compensation philosophy; (f) reviewing and approving executive compensation in a manner that qualifies for the rebuttable presumption of reasonableness under the intermediate sanctions rules; (g) reporting its decisions and rationale to the full board; (h) assuring that compensation information is fully and fairly disclosed on Form 990; and (i) assuring that formal and timely performance assessments are conducted for all senior executives.

Committee support. The well-structured compensation committee also will have the authority to obtain the support necessary to conduct its activities. It is common to have corporate human resources executives and a representative of the Office of General Counsel participate as nonvoting "staff" to the committee. The committee also should be authorized to engage a qualified, independent compensation consultant and other professional advisors (e.g., legal, accounting and tax) as needed.

Developing appropriate compensation arrangements. While it is difficult to describe substantive best practices for compensation programs because every organization is different, it is possible to identify the following procedural best practices that should guide the compensation committee:

1. The committee should establish an annual cycle of meetings and related agendas designed to ensure that it fully discharges its responsibilities. Given the increasing sensitivity and complexity of executive compensation matters, this typically will require three or four committee meetings per year for large, complex organizations.
2. The committee should ensure that it is aware of, and has documentation on, every type of executive compensation, benefit and retirement arrangement within the organization.
3. All committee members should receive a complete orientation regarding the organization's executive compensation process and all elements of the executive compensation program.
4. Committee members should receive regular updates on best compensation practices and trends, such as timely articles and technical updates from the organization's general counsel or external advisors. Committee members should also be encouraged to attend formal education conferences on compensation.
5. Committee members should receive timely and comprehensive materials relative to compensation arrangements well in advance of meetings. For each item under consideration, committees should receive a summary of key issues, competitive practice data, recommendations, cost implications and relevant background material from outside corporate advisors.
6. The committee should use competitive practice data prepared by firms that reflect comparable organizations and jobs.
7. In reviewing the substance of a proposed executive compensation arrangement, the committee should consider the circumstances under which an executive will be paid the most for the least value to the organization.
8. When the committee is in final deliberations, it should meet in executive session.
9. Meeting minutes must be prepared and approved before the next committee meeting (or within 60 days after the committee's final action). It may be prudent to request legal counsel to

Additional Best Practice Recommendations

Exempt organizations are facing a heightened level of scrutiny regarding executive compensation. To prepare for this unavoidable surveillance, the compensation committee may wish to consider the following additional best compensation practices:

1. Assess the organization's overall performance before approving annual compensation adjustments.
2. Ensure that management's representation of organizational performance is accurate and well-supported with objective data.
3. Ensure that the market comparability data on which the committee is relying represent all elements of compensation for what truly are comparable jobs in comparable organizations.
4. Involve the general counsel in the committee process to help ensure proper coordination of legal and governance compliance issues.
5. Ensure strong business, strategic and charitable mission support for compensation levels exceeding a predetermined level of market data.
6. Consider using the corporate organization's Web site to communicate compensation matters to the company's public constituency.
7. Avoid addressing issues on a "crisis" basis and consider instead making decisions on significant compensation matters over the course of committee meetings.
8. Adhere to methodologies, performance criteria and results agreed upon before the beginning of the performance period.
9. Describe to all stakeholders each component of the executive compensation program in a manner that is understandable and concise.
10. Act on the reasonable assumption that all actions of the committee will at some point become public.

serve as secretary to the committee and draft the minutes. To avoid interim sanctions, the minutes must include:
- The terms and date of the approved compensation
- The committee members present during discussion of the arrangement and those who voted on it
- The comparability data used and how they were obtained
- Actions taken by committee members who might have a conflict of interest regarding the arrangement under review
- The rationale for determining why executives' compensation might exceed that of a comparable organization or market
10. The committee should regularly report its actions to the full board and be prepared to communicate to other interested parties on the organization's executive compensation program.

By following these best practices, the not-for-profit health care organization and its governing board will be better able to provide fair compensation to its executives while furthering the organization's charitable purposes, keeping the trust of the community it serves and meeting its legal obligations.

Index

A
Accord Limited, 96–97
Accountability, 77
Acquisitions, 72
Action plan, 12
Active communication, 62
Advocating for community, 48–49
Agendas, deadline-driven, 3
Allen, Etta, 91–93, 94, 98, 100
American College of Healthcare Executives, 31, 73
American Hospital Association's Committee on Governance (COG), 37
Annual incentive, 128
Anticipatory plan in succession planning, 15–16
Attitude, nonjudgmental, 25
Audit committee, structuring of, 85–86

B
Balance of power, between board and the chief executive officer, 52–53
Balanced Budget Amendment, 60
Baldwin, Garza, 102–103
Baptist Medical Center (Oklahoma City), 76
Base salary, 127, 128
Bayfront Medical Center (St. Petersburg, Florida), 62, 64–65, 67
Behavior, principles for encouraging sincere, spontaneous, 24–28
Behavioral competencies, 4
Behavioral interpretations, choosing to make, over content interpretation, 22–23
Behavioral leadership model, 4
Benefits, 128
  executive, 129
Bennett, Christopher, 116–117, 126–127
Best practice standard, 131–132, 140
Biggs, Errol, 98, 100
Board
  executive sessions of, 37–44
  guidance from interim chief executive officer, 32–33
  questions to ask chief executive officer, 45–49
  responsibility for succession planning, 3–4
  volunteer status of, 52

Board chair
    coaching as responsibility of, 54–55
    communication with chief
        executive officer, 54–55
    difference between chief executive
        and, 96–97
    questions for the chief executive
        officer, 93
    synergy in chief executive officer
        relationship and, 101–111
Board executive compensation
    committees, recommended
    practices for, 131–139
Boswell, Bill, 103
Brennan, Ann, 94, 97, 98, 100
Brody, Sue, 62, 64
Budrys, Ray, 64, 68
Burgin, Robert F., 101–103, 104, 106,
    108, 109, 110–111
Burnout, 71
    chief executive officer, 72, 75
Bush, George W., 59

C

Calibration of executive
    compensation, 121–130
Capitation, 86–87
Captain-of-industry model of hospital
    chief executive officer, 61–62
Catholic Health East, 73–74
Centegra Health System (Woodstock,
    Illinois), 126–127
Centura Health System (Denver), 60
Charting skill of executive, 5
Chief executive officers (CEOs)
    board chair questions of, 93
    burnout of, 72, 75
    communication with board chair,
        91–100
    competency models in informing
        selection, 8
    difference between board chair
        and, 96–97
    effective review of, 117–118
    efforts to keep current, 74–75
    evaluating leadership of, 66
    financial pressures on, 76
    financial skills of, 60
    flexibility and adaptability of, 77
    interviewing in recruitment of,
        21–29
    length of time of effectiveness,
        68–69
    listening by, 79–88
    managing transition, 31–33
    measurement and evaluation of,
        115–119
    prerequisite skills of, 59–69
    qualities of, 63
    questioning loyalty of, 106
    questions to ask, 45–49
    relationship with board chair,
        103–107
    shortage of candidates for, 71–78
    short-staffed versus shortsighted,
        71–78
    sources of, 66–68
    succession planning in recruitment
        of, 3–19
    synergy in board chair relationship
        and, 101–111
    10-step process for determining
        compensation for, 127–130
    tenure of, as structural issue, 68
    time table in, 68–69
    turnover of, 31
    typical path for, 72
Chief financial officers (CFOs), 86–88
Chief transformation officer, 80
Coaching as responsibility of board
    chair, 54–55
Coalescence, 43
Columbus (Ohio) Children's Hospital,
    76
Commitment, inspiring, 5
Communication, 7, 69
    active, 62
    crisis, 14
    effective, 33
    in executive sessions, 37–44
    importance of, 88
    knowledge of job in, 98–100

Index

listening in, 79–88
openness and honesty in, 92, 96–98
plan for, 12
questions in, 93
role adjustment in, 96–97
in successful CEO–board chair partnership, 91–100
write-down issues in, 91–92
Community, advocating for, 48–49
Compassion, 107–108
Compensation
 base salary in, 127, 128
 for chief executive officers
  calibration of, 121–130
  committee in determining, 131–139
  three P's in, 115–119
 fee-for-service, 87
 for health care trustees, 52
 incentives in, 12, 123
 philosophy statement in, 132–136
Compensation committee, 131–139
 philosophy statement for, 132–136
 structure and function, 136–139
Competencies, identifying, 14–15
Competency models
 in informing chief executive officer selection, 8
 primary dimensions, 4–8
Consistency, 69
Constructive criticism, 109
Consumer-paid health care, market share of, 47
Content, behavioral interpretations versus, of interview, 22–23
Content interpretation, choosing to make behavioral interpretation over, 22–23
Contingency plans, 14
Continuity of management, 75
Courage, 109
Craven Regional Medical Center (New Bern, North Carolina), 64, 68
Crisis communications, 14

Crisis management policy, 48
Customer service, 76

D

Davis, Larry, 64–65, 66
Deadline-driven agendas, 3
Design and review, 125–126
Diagnosis-related groups (DRGs), 60
Direct reporting relationships, 7
Dye, Carson, 71–72, 73, 74–75

E

Eastman, Brent, 84–85
Employees
 in evaluating chief executive officer leadership, 66
 satisfaction of, 116
Energy, 69
Enron, 121
Ethical foundations of organization's relationships, 48
Executive benefits, 129
Executive compensation, 113
 calibrating, 121–130
 chief executive officer measurement and evaluation, 115–119
 procedure for designing and reviewing, 125–126
Executive sessions, 37–44
 benefits of regular, 53–55
 key purpose of, 44
 limiting of, to one topic, 42
 reasons for, 41
 as standard operating procedure, 51–55
 standard policy on calling, 39
Executive team, focus on, 32
Exempla Healthcare, 42
Experience, identifying, 14–15

F

Fee-for-service compensation, 87
Financial benchmarks, 116
Financial performance and quality-of-care standards, 32

Financial pressures on chief executive officers, 76
First Health, 65
Focus, 69
Forced togetherness, 104–105
Fort Washington (Maryland) Medical Center, 43
Friendship criteria, 117

G

Georgia-Pacific Corp., 73
Giuliani, Rudy, 59
Golden handcuffs, 12
Good Shepherd Health Care System (Hermiston, Oregon), 40–41
Governance consultants, 91
Grow-your-own-CEO philosophy, 75

H

Haeder, Richard, 38–39
Hannan, David, 60, 64, 67, 69
Health care
  public policy development in, 49
  redesign of delivery, 47–48
  skyrocketing cost of, 73, 121
Health care trustees, compensation for, 52
HealthSouth, 121
High-performance relationships, barriers to, 109–111
Hinton, Jim, 61, 64, 66–67
Hiring decisions, 22
Hofer, Sister Kathleen, 95, 98
Hogan, Ron, 73–74, 77
Holy Cross Hospital (Chicago), 65
Honesty, 92, 96–98
Hospital–medical staff relations, 116
Humility, 64

I

Incentives in compensation, 12, 123
Independent auditor, 85
In-depth interviews, 4

Influencing, 5, 7
Information, sharing, 106–107
Innovation, management encouragement of, 47–48
Integrity, 69, 108–109
Interim chief executive officer
  effectiveness of, 31
  guidance from board to, 32–33
Interim management plan, 31–32
Intermediate sanctions, 123–124
Internal candidates, evaluating, 15
Internal Revenue Service (IRS) Tax Form 990, 121–122, 127, 135
Interview, 21–28
  analysis of transcripts, 4
  content versus behavioral interpretations, 22–23
  in-depth, 4
  in recruiting chief executive officer, 21–29

J

Job
  descriptions of, 104
  knowledge of, 98–100
Johnson, Van, 99

K

Kazemek, Ed, 96–97
Keillor, Garrison, 125–126
Kieffer, Witt, 71, 73
Kline, Larry, 81, 82, 85
Knowledge, identifying, 14–15
Kurcz, Lottie, 65, 68–69
Kuypers, Arnie, 72, 74, 75, 76–77
Kuypers Company, 72

L

Lake Wobegon Effect, 125–126
Lame-duck scenario, 14, 19
Leadership
  definitions of, 60
  listening in, 79–88
  paving way for new, 15–17

Index

teaching skills, 78
transition of, 3
Listening, leadership by, 79–88

M

Managed care, 60
Management, ineffective, 21
Marin General Hospital (Greenbrae, California), 91–93, 94, 99
Market share, capturing and holding, 47
Master's in business administration (MBA), 73, 76
Master's in health administration (MHA), 73, 76
McDonald, Virgil, 43
Medical executive committees (MECs), 84
Medical staff
 conflicts with, 68
 in evaluating chief executive officer leadership, 67
Meeting before the meeting, 7
Memorial Health System (South Bend, Indiana), 75–76
Mergers, 72
Michie, Thaine, 93, 95, 96, 100
Micromanaging, 39
Minding the shop mentality, 32
Mission St. Joseph's Health System (Asheville, North Carolina), 101, 108
Moose on the table, 119
Morgan Healthcare Consulting, 71
Mutual growth, 108

N

Newbold, Phil, 75–76, 78
Nonjudgmental attitude, 25
Not-for-profit health care sector, 121

O

One-size-fits-all model of hospital leadership, 68
Openness, 92, 96–98
Operating procedure, executive sessions as standard, 51–55
Orlando (Florida) Regional Healthcare System, 61
Owen, Charles D., III, 104, 106

P

Panarist, Frank, 81–82, 82
Pappelbaum, Stanley, 80–81
Parking lot conversations, movement into boardroom of, 54
Past performance, selection of chief executive officer on basis of, 22
Patient care activities, use of money earned from, 46
Patient satisfaction, 116
Pay-for-performance approach, 130
Pay raises, 75
Performance appraisals, 11, 16, 72–73
Perquisites, 128
Person, Peter, 95, 96–97
Perspective, building shared, 107
Physician leadership cabinet, 83–86
Physicians' relations committee, 41
Policy
 setting, 41–42
 standard, 39–41
Politics, 117, 119
Poudre Valley Health System (Fort Collins, Colorado), 93, 95, 100
Practical Governance, 98
Presbyterian Healthcare Services (Albuquerque, New Mexico), 61, 62
Press, Christopher, 71, 72–73
Prior poor relationship, 109–110
Process, 116–117
Project Scripps, 80–81, 83, 86–87
Promotion decisions, 22
Public policy development in health care, 49
Purpose, establishing, in succession planning, 10–11

Q

Quality-of-care metrics, 116
Quality standards, protecting, 46
Questions
  asking broad general, 25–26
  asking probing, 26–27

R

Rally the troops, 4
Redesign, 47–48
References
  checking of, 65
  importance of, 65
Relationships
  assessment of, 105
  managing key, 48
Reserve accounts, status of, 46
Restructure and redesign, 47–48
Results orientation, 77
Retreat, 40–41
Revenue cycle management, 87
Revenues, managing against declining, 46
Rindler, Michael, 61–62, 68
Rindler Group (Hilton Head, South Carolina), 61–62
Risk, managing against increasing, 46
Roles, clarifying, 103–105
Rothberger, Richard, 86

S

Sabin, Margaret, 91–93, 94, 98, 100
Sabotage, 110
St. Joseph's Health System (Atlanta), 73
St. Mary's/Duluth Clinic Health System (Duluth, Minnesota), 95, 96–97, 98
Salary, base, 127, 128
Sanctions, intermediate, 123–124
Sarbanes-Oxley Act, 38–39, 51
Scandal, avoiding, 131–139
Scripps Clinic, 87
Scripps Health (San Diego, California), 79–88
Secrecy, perception of, 40
Selberg, Jeffrey, 42–44
Self-management, 8
Sexual harassment, 38
Sherman, Mark, 82, 84, 85
Smallmon, John, 40–41
Softer skills, 69
South Shore Hospital (South Weymouth, Massachusetts), 60
Southwestern Vermont Health Care, 54
Stacey, Rulon, 39, 93, 95, 96, 100
Standard policy, 39–41
Stevens, Jack, 110–111
Strack, Gary, 61, 64, 68
Strategic goals, reviewing, in succession planning, 11
Strategic planning fund, 81
Strategic plans, getting buy-in for, 5
Strategic thinking, 116
Strauss, Tom, 91, 94, 100
Structuring the work environment, 7
Success profile, identifying, 14–15
Succession, 76–77
Succession planning
  anticipatory plan in, 15–16
  case for, 9–10
  case studies, 16–18
  components in, 12
  establishing purpose in, 10–11
  initiating, 11
  model for, 3–8
  reviewing strategic goals, 11
  transitional plan, 14–15
  unexpected emergency plan, 12–14
Succession profile, 12
Summa Health System (Akron, Ohio), 91, 94, 97–98, 99
Supplemental Executive Retirement Plans (SERPs), 12, 75, 127, 129, 130
Supply and demand, laws of, 125–126
Sutter Health System (California), 99
Swedish, Joe, 60–61

Index

Synergy in board chair and chief executive officer relationship, 101–111

T

Team building, 69
360-degree feedback process, 16, 65, 130
Three P's, 115–119
Time
    in anticipatory plan, 15
    structuring, 105–106
    in succession planning, 10
    in transition plan, 14
Tone of voice, 28
Totten, Mary, 92
Totten & Associates (Oak Park, Illinois), 92
Transitional plan in succession planning, 14–15
Turnover, chief executive officer (CEO), 31
Tyco, 121
Tyler, Larry, 71, 77–78
Tyler & Company, 71

U

Unexpected emergency plan in succession planning, 12–14

V

Van Gorder, Chris, 81, 82–84
Vision, 61–62, 69
Volunteer status of health care boards, 52

W

Walker, Larry, 39–40, 41–42, 99
Walker Company, 39–40, 99
Wall, Doug, 37–38
Whispering, 37
Work relationships, skill in developing, 7
Working backward, 3
Working from the outside in, 103–107
Working on the inside, 107–109
WorldCom, 121
Write-down issues, 91–92

Y

Yorke, Harvey, 53–54

Trustee

Special Offer for
Better CEO-Board Relations
purchasers.

The official publication of AHA's Center for Healthcare Governance

Lead Your Governing Board to Success!

Health care system and hospital boards need leadership information as they work to improve community health and run financially stable institutions. *Trustee* magazine alerts board members to health care trends that will affect their organization. A wide range of articles will advise them on how to enhance governance skills and better understand executive management and physician concerns. Plus, three times a year, *Trustee* includes a "primer" crafted to provide a solid understanding of a critical health care issue - such as financial investing or information technology. Quarterly supplements also promote skills that can be used at board meetings, retreats and orientations.

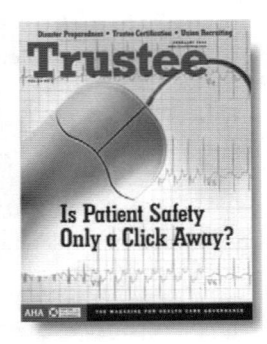

Subscribe Now!

Please order a *Trustee* subscription for each board member. To subscribe, complete this form, sign it and mail it today.

Name (please print) _____

Title (required) _____

Institution _____

Address _____

City _____ State _____ Zip _____

Country _____

Telephone # _____ Fax # _____

E-mail address _____

Signature (required) _____ Date _____

Check appropriate boxes:

☐ United States $49 per year   ☐ Bill me
☐ Canada and Foreign $72 per year (must be prepaid in U.S. dollars)
☐ My check is enclosed, payable to *Health Forum, Inc.* Mail to Health Forum, Attn: Circulation Deptment,
                        1 North Franklin Street, 28th Floor, Chicago, IL 60606-9941.

Please indicate your title:

☐ Chairman (04)   ☐ Governing Board President (05)   ☐ Vice Chairman (09)
☐ Vice President of Board (10)   ☐ Treasurer of Board (15)   ☐ Secretary of Board (20)
☐ Other Board Member (25)   ☐ Other (99) _____

From time to time, *Trustee* and its partners may use information provided on your subscription/renewal card to offer you pertinent industry information.   ☐ I prefer not to receive this information.